GETTING STARTED WITH RUSSIAN

Beginning Russian for Homeschoolers
and Self-Taught Students of Any Age

WILLIAM E. LINNEY

LUCILE H. MCKAY

ARMFIELD ACADEMIC PRESS

© 2024 William E. Linney and Lucile H. McKay

All rights reserved. No part of this book may be used or reproduced by any means graphic, electronic, or mechanical, including photocopying, recording, taping, or by any information storage or retrieval system without the written permission of the copyright holder.

Published by Armfield Academic Press

Editorial consultants: Dr. Robert Fradkin, Sergey Prokofyev

Editorial assistants: Katherine L. Bradshaw, Michelle Yancich

ISBN: 978-1-62611-014-4

CONTENTS

Preface iv

How to Use This Book vi

Lessons 1–151 1

Answer Key 247

Glossary 269

PREFACE

My first book, *Getting Started with Latin*, was a labor of love. I wrote it to help homeschooled and self-taught students learn beginning Latin at home, without a teacher. Since the publication of *Getting Started with Latin*, the response has been positive (except for that one nasty email I got a few years back). People seem to like the one-thing-at-a-time format of the book, which never leaves them lost and wondering what just happened, like other books do. This is significant because homeschooled and self-taught students are a special group of people who need specialized materials—products that allow them to learn at home without access to a teacher who specializes in that particular subject.

After *Getting Started with Latin*, my friend Antonio Orta and I wondered if we could apply that same one-thing-at-a-time approach to a modern language such as Spanish, and so *Getting Started with Spanish* was born. Then, a few years later, Brandon Simpson and I wrote *Getting Started with French* and *Getting Started with German*. Now, along with my co-author Lucile McKay, I present to you *Getting Started with Russian*.

Like its predecessors, *Getting Started with Russian* is designed to accomplish several educational goals. We have designed this book to…

- Be self-explanatory, self-paced, self-contained, and inexpensive
- Allow the student to make progress with or without a teacher
- Provide plenty of practice exercises after each new concept so that the student can master each idea before moving on to the next one
- Provide audio recordings for aural practice and supplementary instruction
- Avoid making Russian any more difficult than it actually is

Getting Started with Russian was created to meet the unique needs of homeschooled and self-taught students. It is self-contained, with no extra materials to purchase (such as pronunciation recordings, answer keys, or teachers' editions). It's also in a large format to make it easier to use, and non-consumable (that is, you aren't supposed to write in it) so it can be used with multiple children. The answer key is in the back of the book, and there are free pronunciation recordings and authors' commentary recordings available at the following website:

www.GettingStartedWithRussian.com

In this book, new words and concepts are introduced in a gradual yet systematic fashion. Each lesson provides many exercises for practicing the new material while reviewing material from previous lessons.

Getting Started with Russian makes Russian accessible to students of any age or educational background. Because this book moves so gradually, you probably will not say *This is too hard for me. I quit!* Instead, these bite-size lessons leave you encouraged and ready to continue. But when you do finish this book, don't let your Russian studies end there. Learning and using a foreign language is quite a thrill—so keep going, and above all, have fun with it!

William E. Linney

HOW TO USE THIS BOOK

This book is structured around one main teaching method: Teach one concept at a time and let the student master that concept before introducing the next one. With that in mind, read the tips listed below to help you use this book to the greatest advantage.

THE NEW WORD

Start each lesson by observing the new word for that particular lesson. All Russian words in this book will, of course, be in the Russian alphabet, but also in **bold print** so they will be easy to find at a glance. The meaning of the new word is in *italics*. In some lessons you will learn a new concept and in others you will simply review material from previous lessons.

PRONUNCIATION

The best way to learn correct pronunciation is by listening and copying what you hear. Visit www.GettingStartedWithRussian.com to hear the free pronunciation recordings. In these recordings, each new word and exercise is read aloud so you can not only read, but also hear, the exercises. These free audio recordings will help you achieve proper pronunciation and provide you with lots of opportunities for aural translation practice.

If needed, there will be a written pronunciation tip at the beginning of a particular lesson. These tips are there to give you a general idea of how the word sounds and to help you avoid the most likely pronunciation errors.

GRAMMATICAL INFORMATION

If needed, a lesson may contain an explanation of how to use the new word introduced in that lesson. Charts and examples are used to give the reader a clear understanding of the grammar knowledge needed to translate the exercises for that particular lesson.

The book's website has special audio commentary recordings which have been prepared by the authors. These recordings discuss each lesson, so if you have any trouble understanding the material presented in a lesson, you will have plenty of help on hand.

THE EXERCISES

Armed with the knowledge of the new word and how to use it, begin to translate the exercises. In a homeschool environment, it is probably best to have students write their answers in a notebook. Older students and adults may prefer to do the exercises mentally. Next, turn to the answer key to see if your translations are correct. In the paperback version of the book, the answer key is in the back. In the Kindle version, the answers are immediately after the lesson, on the next page. By comparing the exercises and the answers, you will learn from your mistakes. Translating the exercises over and over (even memorizing them) will enhance learning and speed your progress. After you have translated the exercises and you know what they mean, listen to the audio recordings over and over for practice. The more you listen, the faster your progress will be.

REPEATED LISTENING

After you have studied the exercises and you know what they mean, you are in a position to use an extremely effective language-learning technique. This technique involves reading or hearing understandable material in the foreign language that you are studying. If you are studying a foreign language, and you hear or read lots of material that you can't understand, it doesn't really do you any good. But if you hear or read something that is at your current level of learning, you are getting some good practice interpreting that language because the material is understandable.

Here's how this applies to you: once you have studied the exercises for a certain lesson, and you know what the exercises mean, you should listen to the audio recordings for that lesson over and over. Don't just listen once or twice—listen to them a hundred times, until everything you hear sounds natural to you. Listen in the car, while cleaning up, etc. This study method will help your brain to process, absorb, and get used to the language.

PRACTICING CONVERSATIONAL SKILLS

Once you understand the exercises, it's time to practice using what you have learned. The ideal situation would be to have a family member or friend with whom you can practice simple conversations on a daily basis. Repetition is the key here. Try repeating the exercises over and over to each other, or making up your own similar sentences.

If you can't practice with a friend or family member, you can still accomplish a lot on your own. You can practice your pronunciation skills by trying to pronounce the exercises just like the speaker. You can practice your listening skills by repeatedly listening to and interpreting the recordings. Or, you can create your own sentences using the vocabulary you have learned. Some language learners practice by speaking to their pets—the family cat won't mind listening to you for a few minutes between naps.

RUSSIAN COMPOSITION

For an additional challenge, you can try to translate the answers to the exercises from English back into Russian using the knowledge you have gained from that lesson. This is a great learning tool because it requires you to think about the material from a completely different direction. Try it and see! Again, it is probably best to write these exercises in a notebook.

DON'T PUT THE CART BEFORE THE HORSE

Do not skip ahead to a future lesson. Because each lesson builds directly on the preceding lessons, do the lessons in the order given. If you start to feel lost or confused, back up a few lessons and review. Or, take a break and come back to the material at a later time. Remember that review and repetition are essential when learning any language. One of the best things you can do to improve your understanding of this new language is to review the lessons repeatedly.

STAY FLEXIBLE

Everyone has a different learning style, so use this book in ways that fit your needs or the needs of your students. You can learn as a family, on your own, or in a homeschool environment. Be creative! You could even have one night of the week when the entire family is forbidden to speak English! Who knows? You may think of a way to use this book that no one else has thought of (putting it under the short leg of the kitchen table does not count).

TESTS AND QUIZZES

To give a student a test or quiz, simply back up to a previous lesson and have the student translate those exercises without looking at the answers. Then, the teacher or parent can grade the exercises using the answers in the back of the book. Another possibility would be to test the student's listening skills by having the student translate the exercises directly from the audio recording for that lesson.

SCHEDULING

Some homeschool parents like a lot of structure in their teaching schedules, while others prefer a less structured learning environment. Depending on your personal preferences, you may either plan to cover a certain number of lessons in a certain period of time, or allow your students to determine their own pace. It's up to you.

HOW MUCH TIME PER DAY?

A few minutes a day with this book is better than longer, less frequent sessions. Thirty minutes a day is ideal for language study. Of course, this may vary with each student's age, ability, and interest level.

SELF-TAUGHT ADULTS

Adults who use this book will enjoy the freedom of learning whenever and wherever they please. High school and college students may use it to get a head start before taking a traditional class at their school, to satisfy curiosity, or to try something new. Busy adults may use it to study at lunchtime, break time, or while commuting to work (as long as someone else is driving the vehicle). The short lessons in this book will fit any schedule.

SURF THE INTERWEBS!

Don't forget about the website that accompanies this book. Here's that web address again, in case you missed it:

www.GettingStartedWithRussian.com

It has free resources to aid you in your studies. Be sure to check it out!

LESSON ONE

THE RUSSIAN ALPHABET AND YOU

Languages start out as spoken words, not as written texts. If you want to write down a language, you'll need some kind of writing system. As English speakers, we write down our language with an alphabet. Each letter makes a different sound, and we can use these letters to spell out the words of our language.

Just for fun, here's a quick overview of how our alphabet developed (use the numbers to follow along with the map of the Mediterranean Sea that is provided below). It all started way back in ancient Egypt, the land of the pyramids and the Nile River (1). The Egyptians used special symbols called *hieroglyphs* to write the Egyptian language on statues, monuments, and on the walls of tombs and temples. It's a long story, but some of these Egyptian characters were used to create an early alphabet for languages related to Hebrew. Archaeologists have found inscriptions using this early alphabet in the Sinai Peninsula (2). This early alphabet traveled to Palestine (3), where it was used by various groups of people. The Phoenicians were sea merchants who were based in what today would be Lebanon (4). As they sailed all over the Mediterranean Sea, they took this alphabet with them. The ancient Greeks (5) borrowed this alphabet from the Phoenicians, made a few changes, and used it to write down the ancient Greek language. The Romans (6), with some help from their Etruscan neighbors, adapted the Greek alphabet for Latin. Over the centuries, as the Roman Empire and the

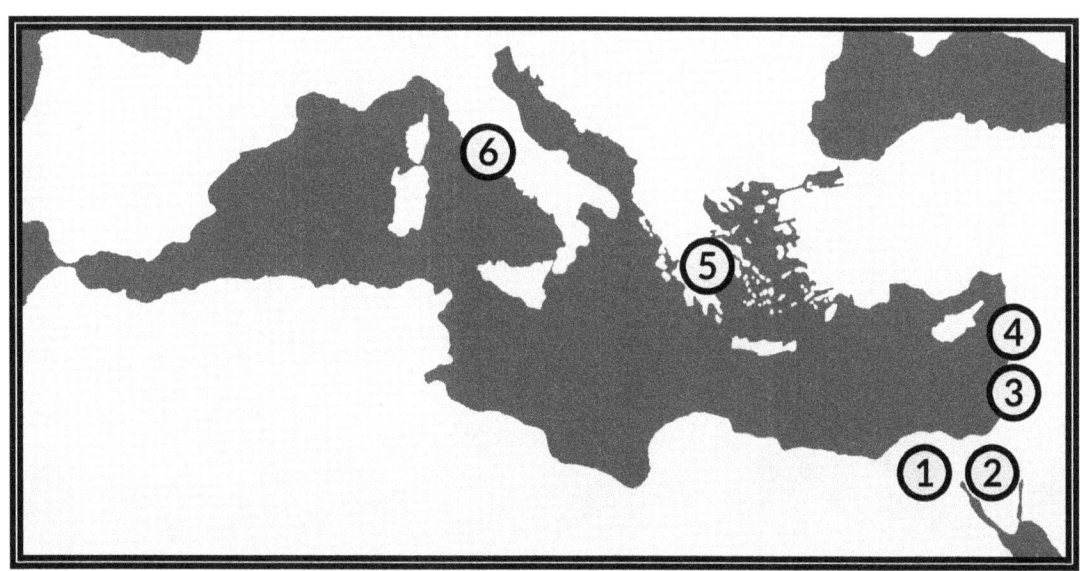

Christian religion spread throughout Europe, so did the Roman alphabet. As a result, the countries that are predominantly Catholic (and later Protestant) use the Latin alphabet. That's why languages such as Spanish, French, Italian, English, German, and even Scandinavian languages use the Latin alphabet. This is also true for Hungarian and some Slavic languages such as Polish, Czech, Slovenian, and Croatian. But other Slavic languages such as Russian, Ukrainian, Bulgarian, and Serbian are in areas that are predominantly Eastern Orthodox, and so those languages use the Cyrillic alphabet which is based on the Greek alphabet.

The story of the Russian alphabet is kind of a long one, but here's our attempt at a short version: St. Cyril (c. AD 827–869) and his brother Methodius (c. AD 815–884) were missionaries sent to the Slavic peoples in the ninth century. They wanted to translate the Bible into the Slavic language, but the Slavic language contained certain sounds that could not be represented by existing Greek or Roman letters. To solve this problem, Cyril created a new alphabet for the Slavic language. Cyril's original alphabet was later replaced by a Greek-based alphabet, which was called *Cyrillic* in his honor. This change happened when the South Slavs started using the Greek alphabet to write down their language, but they had to add a few new letters to represent sounds that the Greek alphabet did not have. That was the beginning of the Cyrillic alphabet, the ancestor of today's Russian alphabet. Since the Russian alphabet and the English alphabet are both derived from the Greek alphabet, you might say that they are cousins. For this reason, some of the characters of the Russian alphabet will look familiar to you.

Soooooo…if you want to learn how to read Russian, the first thing you need to do is learn the Russian alphabet. But don't worry—you will learn the letters of the Russian alphabet one at a time over the next few lessons.

LESSON TWO

WRITE THE LETTERS

Learning to read a new alphabet can be difficult—it can feel as if you are a beginning reader, learning to read for the first time. In order to read Russian, your eye must learn how to recognize each letter quickly, and you must remember the pronunciation of each letter so you can sound out words. And, when you're starting out, sometimes you forget the sound a letter is supposed to make!

But there is a good method you can use to help yourself quickly learn the characters of the Russian alphabet: practice writing out the letters by hand. Get yourself a nice pen and some paper, and try to copy each letter exactly. As you write each letter, think about the sound it makes. Later, when you begin to learn entire Russian words, write out the whole words and pronounce them as you write them. If you use this method regularly, you will quickly become familiar with the Russian alphabet and you'll be able to read the exercises in this book.

LESSON THREE

SOME FAMILIAR-LOOKING LETTERS

Many letters of the Russian alphabet will be completely unfamiliar to you. But there are a few Russian letters that look and sound like letters you already know because both the Latin alphabet (the one we use for English) and the Russian alphabet are derived from the Greek alphabet. Let's start your journey toward learning Russian by examining three familiar-looking letters.

This Russian letter below looks and sounds just like the letter *k*. The name of this Russian letter is *ka* (pronounced *kah*).

К

This next letter looks and sounds just like a capital *m*. The name of this letter, like its Latin counterpart, is *em*.

M

And finally, this letter looks and sounds like a capital *t*. The name of this letter is *te* (pronounced *teh*).

T

Congratulations! You now know three letters of the Russian alphabet.

LESSON FOUR

UPPER CASE AND LOWER CASE LETTERS

In English, an upper case letter and its corresponding lower case letter can look very different. For example, observe the upper case and lower case variations of the letter *g*:

G g

But for most of the letters in the Russian alphabet, the lower case form is just a smaller version of the upper case form. For each of the letters we learned in the last lesson, let's compare their upper case and lower case forms.

К к   М м   Т т

See? They look the same. This is good news for you as a student of Russian because it means that there are fewer characters for you to memorize, making it easier to learn the Russian alphabet.

There are only four Russian characters that have different upper and lower case forms, and they are not hard to learn. We will point them out to you when we run into them.

LESSON FIVE

A GIMMICK FOR LEARNING

The goal of the first part of this book is to teach you the letters of the Russian alphabet. You need to be able to recognize each letter and sound it out so that you can read and pronounce Russian words. In order to familiarize you with the Russian letters, we are going to use a special teaching technique…well, perhaps "gimmick" is a more accurate term.

Here's the gimmick: we will give you exercises in which we use Russian letters to spell out English words. Your challenge is to sound out these words, trying to figure out what the English word is supposed to be. As you work through the exercises in each lesson, you will gradually become familiar with most of the Russian alphabet. You will not learn the letters in the order of the Russian alphabet, but in the order in which they are easiest to learn—and spell out a variety of words. This gimmick…er, highly sophisticated teaching method has its limitations, and won't work for every letter—but it's a start! Above all, try to have fun with it and enjoy the learning process.

LESSON SIX

NEW LETTER

A a

LETTER NAME: *ah*
SOUND IT MAKES: the *a* in *father*

Our new letter for this lesson is one of those few letters that has a different upper case and lower case form. These are easy to learn because they look just like the English letter *a*. Later we will tell you more about this letter—but for now, pronounce it like the *a* in *father, pasta,* and *taco*.

Now it's time to start the learning gimmick…er, method in which we spell out English words with Russian letters. Here's how we will do it: let's say that we wanted to spell out the English word *mom* with Russian letters. We could start with the letter **м** *(em)*, then put the letter **а** *(ah)*, and then the letter **м** *(em)* again, like this:

мам

It's important to remember that the letter **а** *(ah)* sounds like the *a* in *father*. If you pronounce it some other way, the word you are reading will end up sounding like a different word such as *ma'am* or *maim*.

Here's another example—let's see if we can spell out the word *mock*. Let's start with the letter **м** *(em)*, then an **а** *(ah)*, and then a **к** *(kah)*.

мак

If you pronounce the **а** *(ah)* like the *a* in *father*, the word sounds like the English word *mock*.

By now you get the idea. So, stick with us for a few lessons, read and sound out all the practice exercises, and soon you'll know the Russian alphabet well enough to move forward in your studies. Hopefully this interactive learning method will be both fun and educational for you.

LESSON SEVEN

NEW LETTER

П

LETTER NAME: *peh*
SOUND IT MAKES: the *p* in *pizza*

Our new letter for this lesson is an example of one of the many Greek letters that the Russian alphabet is based on. You may have seen this Greek letter in your math studies. It is called *pi* and it looks like this:

In the math world, this character represents the value 3.1416, which is the number of times the diameter of a circle can fit around the circumference of a circle.

In the exercises below, can you find words such as *mop, pot, cop, papa, pop, mom, Tom,* and *mama*? Don't forget to pronounce the letter **a** *(ah)* like the *a* in *father*.

Also note that in Russian, as in English, a person's name is capitalized.

READING PRACTICE (ENGLISH WORDS)

1. мап
2. пат
3. кап
4. папа
5. пап
6. мам
7. Там
8. мама

Answers on page 247.

LESSON EIGHT

NEW LETTER

LETTER NAME: *ee*
SOUND IT MAKES: the *ee* in *meet*

Our new letter for this lesson will look completely unfamiliar to you. It looks like a backward capital *N*, or maybe like a capital *H* with a diagonal line instead of a horizontal one. You'll have to get accustomed to the fact that this letter sounds like the *ee* in *meet*.

In the exercises below, can you find words such as *me, key, team,* and *meet*? And when you are finished, turn to the answer key and try to write out those English words with Russian letters.

READING PRACTICE (ENGLISH WORDS)

1. ми
2. ки
3. тим
4. мит
5. кип
6. типат
7. кап
8. пат
9. мап
10. пап

Answers on page 247.

LESSON NINE

NEW LETTER

Б б

LETTER NAME: *beh*
SOUND IT MAKES: the *b* in *boy*

Our new letter for this lesson is yet another Russian letter from the Greek alphabet. This letter and our English letter *b* were both derived from the Greek letter *beta*, which looks like this in its upper case and lower case forms:

B β

As you can see, the upper case form of the Russian letter *beh* looks like an upper case Greek *beta*, but with part of the top loop removed. This Russian letter is one of those few letters that looks different in its upper case and lower case forms, so be on the lookout for both forms.

In Russian, as in English, a person's name is capitalized. So if we wanted to spell out the English name *Bob*, we would start it out with a capital *beh* and finish it with a lower case *beh* like this:

Баб

In the exercises below, can you find words such as *Bob, bee, beat,* and *beak*? Don't forget: when you are finished sounding out the exercises, write out the English answers in Russian letters.

READING PRACTICE (ENGLISH WORDS)

1. Баб	4. бик	7. тим	10. пик
2. би	5. бип	8. типат	11. мит
3. бит	6. ми	9. ки	12. Там

Answers on page 247.

LESSON TEN

NEW LETTER

С

LETTER NAME: *es*
SOUND IT MAKES: the *s* in *sailor*

At first glance, you might think that our new letter for this lesson is somehow related to our letter *c*, but that's only a coincidence. It's a long story, but it's actually a certain form of the Greek letter *sigma*. Over the centuries, the letter *sigma* has been written in a variety of ways, such as these:

$$\Sigma \quad \sigma \quad s \quad \varsigma \quad c$$

Notice that sometimes the tail of the *sigma* is longer, making the letter look like our letter *s*. Other times, the tail is small, and other times there is no tail at all! So you see, this Greek letter is the source of both our letter *s* and the Russian letter **с** *(es)* which has no tail. So if you find it helpful, you could think of the letter **с** *(es)* as an *s* with no tail.

In the exercises below, can you find words such as *seat, steep, seek,* and *steam*?

READING PRACTICE (ENGLISH WORDS)

1. сит
2. стип
3. сик
4. стим
5. спатс
6. пис
7. бист
8. сим
9. бит
10. мапс
11. кип
12. Баб
13. кап
14. митс
15. бик
16. Баби

Answers on page 247.

LESSON ELEVEN

NEW LETTER

LETTER NAME: *ooh*
SOUND IT MAKES: the *oo* in *moon*

Our new letter for this lesson looks just like a lower case *y* and sounds like the *oo* in *moon*.

In the exercises below, can you find words such as *soup, moose,* and *boom*?

READING PRACTICE (ENGLISH WORDS)

1. суп
2. мус
3. бум
4. тим
5. бакс
6. Баб
7. ски
8. митс
9. кап
10. бипс
11. стапс
12. стип
13. пис
14. сик
15. бит
16. сит

Answers on page 247.

LESSON TWELVE

NEW LETTER

LETTER NAME: *tseh*
SOUND IT MAKES: the *ts* in *hits*

The letter **ц** *(tseh)* combines two consonant sounds: *t* and *s*. You can hear this sound combination in English words like *pots*, *meets*, and *beets*, or like the way the two *z*'s sound in the middle of the word *pizza*. In English, we most often find this *ts* sound combination at the end of a word—but in Russian, this sound can happen at the beginning, middle, or end of a word.

Some of you may be familiar with the word *czar*, which means *emperor*. In a governmental context, it can mean someone who is in put in charge of a certain task or department (e.g., "Dr. Smith was the president's immigration czar."). This word originally comes from the word *Caesar*. Julius Caesar's family ruled the Roman Empire for so long that the word *Caesar* eventually became a title for the emperor.

In English, you may see this word spelled as *czar*, but the actual Russian word starts with our new letter for this lesson, so it is more accurately rendered as *tsar*.

In the exercises below, can you find words such as *meets*, *beets*, *spots*, and *teapots*?

READING PRACTICE (ENGLISH WORDS)

1. миц
2. биц
3. спац
4. типац
5. буц
6. мапс
7. кипс
8. Баби
9. ми
10. бик
11. тим
12. сик
13. стап
14. ски
15. сакс
16. бум

Answers on page 247.

13

LESSON 13

NEW LETTER

LETTER NAME: *el*
SOUND IT MAKES: the *l* in *lake*

Our new letter for this lesson started out as the Greek letter *lambda* which (in its lower case form) looks like this:

Be careful not to mix up this letter **л** *(el)* with the letter **п** *(peh)* because they look very similar. The difference is that the letter **л** *(el)* has one "foot" sticking out to the left while the letter **п** *(peh)* has two straight "legs." Compare them side by side below.

л п

In the exercises below, can you find words such as *leap, leak, lost,* and *sleep*?

READING PRACTICE (ENGLISH WORDS)

1. лип
2. лик
3. ласт
4. слип
5. ил
6. скул
7. пац
8. буц
9. пул
10. Баб
11. миц
12. пис
13. суп
14. спац
15. бипс
16. мапс

Answers on page 247.

LESSON 14

NEW LETTER

LETTER NAME: *ef*
SOUND IT MAKES: the *f* in *fish*

Our new letter for this lesson is yet another Greek letter—the letter *phi*, which looks like this in its upper case and lower case forms:

In English we have many words in which the letter combination *ph* sounds like an *f*. These words come to us from ancient Greek: words such as *philosophy*, *pharmacy*, and *symphony*. It's a long story, but in their original Greek spellings, the *ph* part of the word was spelled with the letter *phi*.

In the exercises below, can you find words such as *leaf, fool, beef,* and *flutes*?

READING PRACTICE (ENGLISH WORDS)

1. лиф	6. пац	11. буц	16. бик
2. фул	7. скул	12. сил	17. сиц
3. биф	8. фист	13. ил	18. капс
4. флуц	9. мус	14. пил	19. типац
5. флас	10. бист	15. липс	20. суп

Answers on page 248.

LESSON 15

NEW LETTER

LETTER NAME: *deh*
SOUND IT MAKES: the *d* in *dog*

Our new letter for this lesson started out as the Greek letter *delta*, which in its upper case form looks like this:

Think of our new letter for this lesson as the Greek letter *delta* but with a flat top and little feet at the bottom.

In the exercises below, can you find words such as *food*, *deal*, *feed*, and *seafood*?

READING PRACTICE (ENGLISH WORDS)

1. фуд
2. дил
3. фид
4. сифуд
5. дид
6. фул
7. биф
8. фит
9. лац
10. Баби
11. фиц
12. пац
13. фист
14. сиц
15. буц
16. фил
17. суп
18. мик
19. миц
20. пил

Answers on page 248.

LESSON 16

NEW LETTER

LETTER NAME: *eh*
SOUND IT MAKES: the *e* in *pet*

The sound of this letter is *eh* as in *bet*, *bread*, and *friend*. Be sure not to write this letter like the number 3, because then it will look like a different Russian letter. Instead, make the right side of it rounded, as shown above.

In the exercises below, can you find words such as *fed*, *pest*, *led*, and *pets*?

READING PRACTICE (ENGLISH WORDS)

1. фэд	6. фэл	11. стил	16. буц
2. пэст	7. лэфт	12. лэц	17. Баб
3. лэд	8. спэл	13. сид	18. дил
4. пэц	9. бэлт	14. сэц	19. дац
5. бэц	10. дип	15. фид	20. кул

Answers on page 248.

LESSON 17

NEW LETTER

Н

LETTER NAME: *en*
SOUND IT MAKES: the *n* in *nut*

This letter looks like a capital *H*—but don't be fooled! It started out as the Greek letter *nu* which (in its upper case form) looks like this:

But over the centuries the downward diagonal line in the middle became horizontal, so over time this letter ended up looking more like a capital *H* than a capital *N*. Be careful not to confuse this with the letter **и** (pronounced *ee*) which has an upward-pointing diagonal line.

In the exercises below, can you find words such as *moon*, *nets*, *need*, and *neck*?

READING PRACTICE (ENGLISH WORDS)

1. мун
2. нэц
3. нид
4. нэк
5. дэк
6. бин
7. нэст
8. спун
9. миц
10. стил
11. буц
12. фист
13. пац
14. сид
15. лэд
16. сифуд
17. пул
18. фил
19. сиц
20. фэд

Answers on page 248.

18

LESSON 18

NEW LETTER

LETTER NAME: *yu*
SOUND IT MAKES: the word *you*

This letter is similar to **у** *(ooh)*, which you already know. The difference is that **ю** *you* has a *yuh* sound at the beginning. Also, it looks kind of like a spaceship.

In the exercises below, can you find the words that contain a *you* sound—words like *fuel*, *mule*, and *yule*?

READING PRACTICE (ENGLISH WORDS)

1. фюл
2. мюл
3. юл
4. фюд
5. мют
6. бюти
7. Юта
8. юник
9. фю
10. мэню
11. нэц
12. лэц
13. фэд
14. сэд
15. бэц
16. дац
17. сил
18. биц
19. бэл
20. дид
21. пац
22. сифуд
23. нид
24. сиц

Answers on page 248.

LESSON 19

HARD AND SOFT CONSONANTS

You have learned quite a few Russian consonants so far, and you have many more to learn about. But before we continue teaching you about Russian consonants, we need to tell you about an important concept: the fact that in Russian, certain consonants can be pronounced two different ways. The terms we use to talk about these two ways are *hard* and *soft*. If a consonant is a "hard" consonant, it will have one particular sound, and if a consonant is a "soft" consonant, it will have a different sound.

We have something a little similar to this in English. Take, for example, the letter *g*. In the following two words, compare the sound that the letter *g* makes.

- golf
- germ

The *g* in the word *golf* sounds completely different than the *g* in the word *germ*. So you see, the letter *g* can make two different sounds. In English, we say that the *g* in the word *golf* makes a hard *g* sound, but the *g* in the word *germ* makes a soft *g* sound. The letter *g* is usually hard before the vowels *a, o,* and *u* (or at the end of a word). But *g* is usually soft before the vowels *i, e,* and *y*.

In Russian, as in English, there are certain consonants that can have two different sounds. These sounds are also referred to as hard and soft sounds—but the difference between hard and soft is not the same in Russian as it is in English. So in the next lesson we will start to explore the difference between hard and soft consonants in Russian (and also how to pronounce them with an authentic Russian accent).

LESSON 20

HARD AND SOFT CONSONANTS IN RUSSIAN (PALATALIZATION)

In the last lesson, we told you that certain Russian consonants can have both a "hard" sound and a "soft" sound. It is somewhat similar to the way that the letter *g* works in English, but the pronunciation of soft consonants is different in Russian. Let's take a look now at the specifics of how to pronounce soft consonants in Russian.

Here is the basic idea: in Russian, when a consonant is hard, you will pronounce that consonant generally the same way as you would in English. But when a consonant is soft, you must do something special: raise the middle of your tongue to the roof of your mouth as if you are saying a *yuh* sound, like the beginning of the word *young*. This process of raising the tongue is called *palatalization*. Why is it called that? Take a look at this diagram of the human mouth.

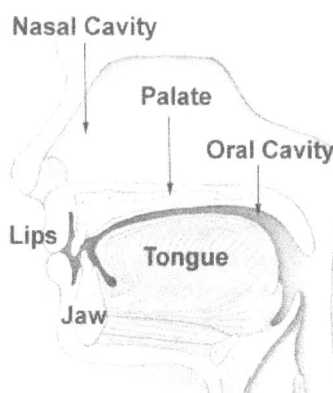

The roof of the mouth, in scientific terms, is called the *palate* (pronounced *PAL-it*). In the front and middle of the mouth, the roof of the mouth is hard, so that part is called the *hard palate*. In the back of your mouth, near the throat, the roof of the mouth is soft, so that part is called the *soft palate* or *velum*.

When a consonant is soft, the center of the tongue is raised up toward the roof, or palate, of the mouth both during and after the articulation of the sound. This raised tongue position blends with the consonant sound and colors the sound of the consonant, giving that consonant a distinctly different quality—and that is what is called *palatalization*.

Let's do a little exercise: pronounce these two words slowly. As you do, take note of where your tongue travels as you say each word.

- food
- feud

Did you notice anything? Here's what we were hoping you would notice: when you say the word *food,* your tongue doesn't do much—it just sits there at the bottom of your mouth. But when you say the word *feud,* the center of your tongue rises to the roof of your mouth—that's the kind of tongue movement that is involved when you pronounce a soft consonant in Russian. When you pronounce a soft consonant, you will raise the middle of your tongue during the pronunciation of the consonant, and that will change the quality of the consonant's sound.

So for now, keep practicing with the words *food* and *feud* until you understand what we are saying about the tongue movements that you make when pronouncing these words. When you have understood this important concept, go on to the next lesson.

LESSON 21

RECOGNIZING HARD AND SOFT CONSONANTS

In the last lesson, we told you that in Russian there are hard and soft consonants. We mentioned that soft consonants are pronounced with a special kind of tongue movement called *palatalization*—that's when you raise the middle of your tongue to the roof of your mouth during the pronunciation of a consonant.

So you may be asking this question: *How do I know if a Russian consonant is hard or soft?* We're glad you asked.

A couple of lessons ago, we talked about the letter *g* in English. We mentioned that sometimes it has a "hard" sound like the *g* in *golf*, and other times it has a "soft" sound like the *g* in *germ*. We also mentioned that certain vowels come after each kind of *g*. For example, if a *g* comes before the letters *a*, *o*, or *u*, it will be a hard *g*, as seen in these examples.

- game
- gate
- golf
- goal
- gum
- gust

But when the letter *g* comes before the letters *e*, *i*, or *y*, it will usually be a soft *g*:

- germ
- gene
- gentleman
- giant
- giraffe
- ginger
- gypsum
- gyroscope

Of course, there will be some exceptions to these rules, and there will be other rules that govern more specific situations—but the point we are trying to make here is that there is a (somewhat) predictable pattern when it comes to the vowels that follow the letter *g*.

In Russian, this same kind of thing happens, but on a larger scale. There are certain vowels in the Russian alphabet that indicate that the previous consonant is hard, while certain other letters (vowels, mostly) indicate that the previous consonant is soft—that is, palatalized, meaning that particular consonant will have a sort of *yi* sound mixed in with it.

Also, there are a few Russian consonants that are always hard, no matter what consonant follows them, and a couple of consonants that are always soft. We will point these out to you as we come across them.

In the next lesson, we will explore Russian vowels a bit more with an eye toward how they affect the pronunciation of consonants.

LESSON 22

RUSSIAN VOWEL PAIRS

Over the last few lessons, we have been taking a break from learning new letters in order to explore hard and soft consonant sounds, as well as the vowels that work with them. For students of Russian, this is extremely important—Russian students need to know that certain letters (vowels, mostly) indicate that the previous consonant will be hard, while other Russian letters indicate that the previous consonant will be soft (palatalized).

The way it works in Russian is that, for each kind of vowel sound, there are two vowels: one that indicates that the consonant immediately before it is hard, and one that indicates that the consonant immediately before it is soft (palatalized). Therefore, those two vowels will form a pair: what we might call the hard-indicating version of that vowel sound, and the soft-indicating version of that vowel sound, for lack of better terms.

Here's an example of what we mean. Think for a moment about the vowel sound found in English words such as *tune, dune,* and *June.* In Russian, we have two vowels that make that kind of vowel sound:

у   **ю**
(ooh)   *(yu)*

Both of these vowels have the same vowel sound, but with one big difference—**у** *(ooh)* indicates that the previous consonant is hard while **ю** *(yu)* indicates that the previous consonant is soft (palatalized). So, you can think of these two vowels as a pair, where one is the hard-indicating one and the other is the soft-indicating one.

As we go along, we will put these vowel pairs into a special chart so that you can compare them. In the left column you will see the basic vowel sound, and then in the other two columns you will see the Russian vowels that are the hard-indicating and soft-indicating versions of that particular vowel sound. In this way, you will be able to envision these two versions of the same sound as counterparts—two sides of the same coin, so to speak.

Here is what the chart would look like right now if we put in all the vowels you know so far.

RUSSIAN VOWEL PAIRS	INDICATES HARD CONSONANT	INDICATES SOFT CONSONANT
the *a* in f*a*ther	**а** *(ah)*	
the *e* in b*e*d	**э** *(eh)*	
the *e* in f*ee*t		**и** *(ee)*
the *o* in c*o*mb		
the *u* in J*u*ne	**у** *(ooh)*	**ю** *(you)*

Again, as we go along, we will add more and more vowels to this chart. When you see them in pairs like that, it will help you understand that there are two versions of each sound.

Before we finish up this lesson, there is one last thing we want to mention. Not every soft-indicating vowel provides the same strength of palatalization. Some of them, such as **ю** *(you)*, add what sounds like a *yi* sound. However, the letter **и** *(ee)* doesn't have a very strong *yi* sound. In fact, you can barely hear it. This is because, when you say that vowel sound (the *ee* in *feet*) your tongue must remain near the roof of the mouth, in the same place as it would be when pronouncing a palatalized consonant. Because the tongue remains parked in generally the same spot, there is no discernible *yi* sound.

And, as we mentioned before, a few consonants are either always hard or soft, and are not affected by the vowel that follows them.

For this reason, we strongly suggest that you listen carefully to the recordings that we have provided, so you can absorb the sounds that we are describing to you. Reading about a language is good, and it's also good to have an intellectual understanding of sound rules and spelling—but this is only to prepare you for the most important step of all, which is using your ears!

LESSON 23

NEW LETTER

LETTER NAME: *shah*
SOUND IT MAKES: the *sh* in *show*

We aren't sure about this, but this letter may have originally come from the Hebrew letter *shin* (pronounced *sheen*), which looks like this:

Coincidence? You be the judge!

In order to represent this kind of sound with English letters, we must use two letters: *s* and *h*. Together, they represent a *sh* sound, like the *sh* in *show*. But, in Russian you can represent this sound with only one letter: **Ш** *(shah)*. The Greek alphabet didn't have a letter that makes a *sh* sound, so that's why this letter may have been borrowed from Hebrew. This consonant is always hard, regardless of what vowel follows it.

In the exercises below, can you find words such as *shed, chef,* and *shock*?

READING PRACTICE (ENGLISH WORDS)

1. шэд	6. бюти	11. фю	16. флуц
2. шэф	7. мэню	12. ист	17. сиц
3. шак	8. мют	13. нэст	18. дун
4. сифуд	9. юник	14. бист	19. бэст
5. Юта	10. ю	15. сэц	20. пул

Answers on page 249.

LESSON 24

NEW LETTER

LETTER NAME: *cheh*
SOUND IT MAKES: the *ch* in *cheap*

In order to represent this kind of sound with English letters, we must use two letters: *c* and *h*. Together, they represent a *ch* sound, like the *ch* in *cheap*. But in Russian you can represent this sound with only one letter: **ч** *(cheh)*.

In the exercises below, can you find words such as *cheek*, *cheats*, *beach*, and *peach*?

READING PRACTICE (ENGLISH WORDS)

1. чик	6. чэст	11. шэд	16. дэск
2. чиц	7. чиф	12. юл	17. фэл
3. бич	8. чэк	13. лин	18. шап
4. пич	9. шэф	14. фюд	19. фуд
5. лич	10. шуц	15. сэл	20. фиц

Answers on page 249.

LESSON 25

STRESSED AND UNSTRESSED SYLLABLES

In this lesson we would like to take another break from introducing new letters so we can explore another important language concept—stressed and unstressed syllables.

In English, when a word has more than one syllable, we generally pronounce one syllable with a bit more emphasis or volume than the other syllables. For example, what syllable gets the emphasis in this word?

> potato

The word *potato* has three syllables. The emphasis or stress is on the second syllable, so it sounds like *puh-TAY-toe*. Therefore we can say that the first syllable is unstressed, the second syllable receives the stress, and the last syllable is unstressed.

Another issue that is related to stress is duration. Not every syllable lasts the same amount of time. Say the word *potato* a few times, and as you do, think about how long each syllable lasts. Which syllable lasts the longest? Which syllable is the shortest?

You probably noticed that the first syllable of this word is much shorter than the other syllables. There are a couple of reasons for this—but the thing we want you to notice here is that this particular syllable is short, and the syllable immediately after it receives the stress. Just as an exercise, pretend that the word *potato* is pronounced with the stress on the first syllable instead of the second syllable *(PUH-tay-toe)*. Pronounce it this way a few times—does it change the duration of the first syllable? Probably so.

One last thing—the duration of a syllable can affect the sound of the vowel in that syllable. Try saying the word *potato* again—say it once the usual way, and then again with the stress on the first syllable. What do you notice about the way the vowel sound in the first syllable changes? Does the vowel sound have the same quality as before? What was the difference?

If you say the word *potato* with the stress on the first syllable, you'll have plenty of time to pronounce it however you wish, and so you might pronounce it like the *po-* at the beginning of the word *poem*. But if you say the word *potato* the usual way, the first syllable lasts a very short time, and mouth takes a shortcut and just says *puh*. In linguistic terms, this quick *uh* vowel sound is called a *reduced vowel*. The reason we are telling you this is because Russian also has reduced vowel sounds.

The Russian language generally isn't written with any kinds of accent marks to indicate what syllable is supposed to get the stress. But often, Russian language materials such as textbooks and dictionaries add in accent marks in order to show which syllable is stressed. And that's what we will do in this book. For example, the Russian word *mashina* means *car*. It has three syllables, and the stress is on the second syllable. So we will write it with an accent mark over the second syllable, like this:

маши́на

That way, you'll be able to see that it sounds something like *mah-SHEEN-uh* or *mah-SHIN-uh*.

So here is the point of this lesson: when a syllable gets the stress, it can change the duration of that syllable, which can change the quality of the vowel for that syllable. As we move forward through this book, we will be telling you about stressed and unstressed vowels in Russian, and how it all affects the pronunciation of Russian words.

LESSON 26

NEW LETTER

LETTER NAME: *ya*
SOUND IT MAKES: the *ya* in *yacht*

Our new letter for this lesson looks like a backwards capital *r*—but don't be fooled! It's really a vowel.

There are two things we need to tell you about this vowel. First of all, this is a soft-indicating vowel, meaning that it tells you that the consonant immediately before it is soft (palatalized). Let's add it to our vowel pair chart along with the previous vowels that we have studied.

RUSSIAN VOWEL PAIRS	INDICATES HARD CONSONANT	INDICATES SOFT CONSONANT
the *a* in f*a*ther	**а** (ah)	**я** (ya)
the *e* in b*e*d	**э** (eh)	
the *e* in f*ee*t		**и** (ee)
the *o* in c*o*mb		
the *u* in J*u*ne	**у** (ooh)	**ю** (you)

The other thing we need to tell you pertains to the sound of this vowel. In the last lesson, we told you that vowels can change their sound depending on whether they are part of a stressed syllable or an unstressed syllable. And that is something you need to keep in mind with **я** *(ya)*. When this vowel is on a stressed syllable, it will sound like *ya*. But when it is on an unstressed syllable, it can become a reduced vowel and it can sound more like *yi* in the word *yippee*.

Let's examine two different Russian words that we can use to demonstrate what we are talking about. First, here is a Russian word in which **Я** *(ya)* is on a stressed syllable. It's the Russian word for *apple*, and it sounds something like *YAHB-luh-kuh*.

я́блоко

Since the first syllable of the word receives the stress, the letter **Я** *(ya)* gets a strong *yuh* sound at the beginning, and sounds like *ya*.

Now compare that to this word in which **Я** *(ya)* is on an unstressed syllable. It is the name of a city in Siberia, and it sounds something like *yi-KUTSK*.

Яку́тск

The letter **Я** *(ya)* is on an unstressed syllable that comes right before the stressed syllable in the word—similar to what happens with the first syllable of the English word *potato*. And that's why **Я** *(ya)* sounds different there.

So the point we are making here is that this vowel can behave differently in different words. So again, as we have said before, make sure to listen carefully to the recordings that we have provided along with this book. When you are a beginning Russian student, you aren't familiar enough with the sounds of the language yet to just trust your eyes and read the word—you also need to use your ears to hear how the words sound when pronounced by a native speaker.

But the primary sound of this vowel is *ya*, and so that's the way we will use it in our reading exercises. We couldn't think of very many English words to spell out with it, but we somehow managed to think of a few. In the exercises below, can you find the words *yacht*, *Maya*, *yon*, and *papaya*?

READING PRACTICE (ENGLISH WORDS)

1. ят	6. чэс	11. син	16. мют
2. Мая	7. бич	12. бюти	17. пул
3. ян	8. чик	13. нид	18. лэфт
4. папая	9. чип	14. шэл	19. шин
5. чит	10. мюл	15. нэст	20. фуд

Answers on page 249.

LESSON 27

NEW LETTER

В

LETTER NAME: *veh*
SOUND IT MAKES: the *v* in *vest*

We promise—we really aren't trying to confuse you! Our new letter for this lesson may look like a capital *b*, but it certainly doesn't sound like one. Furthermore, this letter looks like another letter that you already know—the letter *beh*, which looks like **Б** in its upper case form and **б** in its lower case form. It's a long story—but in a nutshell, both letters came from the Greek letter *beta*.

A quick history lesson: at first, the Greek letter *beta* represented the sound of a *b* like the *b* in *boy*. But over time, the sound of the letter *beta* changed into a *v* sound, like the *v* in *vest*. So when the letter *beta* was absorbed into the Russian alphabet, its *v* sound came along with it—and they had to make a different letter (the letter *beh*) to represent a *b* sound. Both *beh* and *veh* look kinda sorta like the Greek letter *beta*, so don't confuse them!

Let's examine them side by side: on the left we have spelled out the English word *best* with Russian letters, and on the right we have spelled out the word *vest*. Practice reading these two words over and over, and it will help you get accustomed to the difference between *beh* and *veh* before you try the exercises.

бэст (best)   **вэст** (vest)

In the exercises below, can you find words such as *vet, leave, believe,* and *move*? But stay alert—we have mixed in a few words that start with a *b* sound.

READING PRACTICE (ENGLISH WORDS)

1. вэт
2. бэт
3. лив
4. билив
5. мув
6. ян
7. яц
8. Мая
9. вэц
10. чиф
11. ти ви
12. чэст
13. фэч
14. фюд
15. чэк
16. фюл
17. шап
18. бюти
19. нид
20. кин

Answers on page 249.

LESSON 28

NEW LETTER

Г

LETTER NAME: *ghe*
SOUND IT MAKES: the *g* in *golf*

Our new letter for this lesson is really the Greek letter *gamma*, which in its upper case form looks like this:

As we mentioned a few lessons ago, the English letter *g* can have two different sounds—the *g* in *golf* (hard *g*) or the *g* in *germ* (soft *g*). But in Russian, the letter **г** (*ghe*) will always have a hard *g* sound.

In the exercises below, can you find words such as *goose, geese,* and *log*?

READING PRACTICE (ENGLISH WORDS)

1. гус
2. гис
3. лаг
4. пэг
5. эг наг
6. фюд
7. вэст
8. чип
9. билив
10. шац
11. мув
12. папая
13. бич
14. яц
15. чэк
16. пич
17. Юта
18. Мая
19. лич
20. Стив

Answers on page 249.

LESSON 29

NEW LETTER

Е е

LETTER NAME: *yeh*
SOUND IT MAKES: the *ye* in *yell*

This Russian letter is the cousin of our letter *e* because both of them come from the Greek letter *epsilon*. Here's what an *epsilon* looks like in its upper case and lower case forms:

Ε ε

Our new letter for this lesson is a soft-indicating vowel. This means that it indicates that the consonant immediately before it is soft (palatalized). Let's add this letter to our growing vowel pair chart:

RUSSIAN VOWEL PAIRS	INDICATES HARD CONSONANT	INDICATES SOFT CONSONANT
the *a* in f*a*ther	**а** *(ah)*	**я** *(ya)*
the *e* in b*e*d	**э** *(eh)*	**е** *(yeh)*
the *e* in f*ee*t		**и** *(ee)*
the *o* in c*o*mb		
the *u* in J*u*ne	**у** *(ooh)*	**ю** *(you)*

You now know all the Russian letters needed to spell the Russian word for *no*, which sounds like *nyet*. Here's how this word looks in Russian:

нет

The second letter of this word is **е** *(yeh)*, which is our new letter for this lesson. This word is a good one for demonstrating how a palatalized vowel indicates that the previous consonant is soft. In this word, the letter **е** *(yeh)* will indicate that the **н** *(en)* right before it is soft (palatalized), meaning that you will raise the middle of your tongue while you pronounce that consonant sound. This is why the word sounds like *nyet*.

When we use English letters to try to represent Russian words that have palatalization, we will add in a tiny *y* after the palatalized consonant to remind you that it is palatalized. For example, instead of *nyet*, we will put *n^yet*. Hopefully this will help you to remember that the *y* is not a separate *y* sound added after the consonant. Instead, it indicates the palatalization that occurs during, not after, the pronunciation of the consonant. Of course, that's not a perfect way to represent palatalization, but it should work for the purposes of this book.

One last thing before we finish up this lesson: much like we saw with **я** *(ya)* in lesson 26, when **е** *(yeh)* is part of an unstressed syllable, it can have a reduced vowel sound. In that situation, it will be pronounced more like *yi*.

But the primary sound for this letter is the *ye* in *yell*, so that's how we will use it in our exercises. In the exercises below, can you find the words *yet, yell, yes, yeti,* and *yelp*?

READING PRACTICE (ENGLISH WORDS)

1. ет	6. лиг	11. вэст	16. Мая
2. ел	7. гус	12. лив	17. чип
3. ес	8. лэг	13. мув	18. юник
4. ети	9. шэф	14. вэт	19. бич
5. елп	10. бэг	15. ян	20. чиф

Answers on page 250.

LESSON 30

NEW LETTER

LETTER NAME: *yoh*
SOUND IT MAKES: the *yo* in *yoga*

Our new letter for this lesson is called *yoh*. It is really the same letter that we taught you in the last lesson (which looks like an English *e*), except that this one has two dots over it. The dots are there to distinguish it from **е** *(yeh)*.

An important thing to know about this particular letter is that it is *always* on a stressed syllable. So if you ever see this letter out in the wild, you will automatically know what syllable to put the stress on when you pronounce it.

But there is a problem—this letter is not always written with the dots! So you may be wondering—if it doesn't have dots, how do people tell it apart from **е** *(yeh)*? The answer to that question is that native Russian speakers just know from experience how that particular letter is pronounced in various words, whether it has the dots or not. It's similar to the way a native English speaker would know how the letter *a* is pronounced in these two words:

- n<u>a</u>ture
- n<u>a</u>tural

Do the underlined letters sound the same? No—but if a native English speaker sees those words in print, that speaker will know from experience what these words sound like, just from hearing them so many times. And that's how a native Russian speaker knows how the letter **ё** *(yoh)* sounds—regardless of whether it has the dots over it or not.

By the way, this letter fills in yet another space in our growing vowel pair chart.

38

RUSSIAN VOWEL PAIRS	INDICATES HARD CONSONANT	INDICATES SOFT CONSONANT
the *a* in f*a*ther	**а** (ah)	**я** (ya)
the *e* in b*e*d	**э** (eh)	**е** (yeh)
the *e* in f*ee*t		**и** (ee)
the *o* in c*o*mb		**ё** (yo)
the *u* in J*u*ne	**у** (ooh)	**ю** (you)

As you can see from the chart, our new letter for this lesson is the soft-indicating version of the vowel that sounds like the *o* in *comb*. You obviously don't know the hard-indicating version of this vowel sound yet, but you will learn it in the near future.

The letter **ё** *(yoh)* is not very common, so you may not see it in print very often. We don't have any exercises for you for this particular lesson, but you will see the letter **ё** *(yoh)* later in this book when you learn how to say *give* and *go* in Russian. And when we get there, we will be sure to point it out to you!

LESSON 31

NEW LETTER

З

LETTER NAME: *zeh*
SOUND IT MAKES: the *z* in *zebra*

Our new letter for this lesson is really the Greek letter *zeta*, the same letter from which we get our letter *z*. Here's what the Greek *zeta* looks like in its upper case and lower case forms.

Z ζ

Another thing to notice is that our new letter for this lesson looks a lot like another Russian letter that you know—the letter **Э** (*eh*, also known as *backwards e*). Notice that the letter **З** (*zeh*) has an indentation in the right side (like the number 3), while **Э** (*eh*) is flat on the right side. Here they are side by side so you can compare them.

З Э

In the exercises below, can you find words such as *zoo, cheese, zoom,* and *eggs*?

READING PRACTICE (ENGLISH WORDS)

1. зу
2. чиз
3. зум
4. эгз
5. биз
6. лэгз
7. елп
8. ес
9. гус
10. ети
11. лиг
12. бэг

13. гэс	15. билив	17. бич	19. лив
14. папая	16. чэст	18. яц	20. пич

Answers on page 250.

LESSON 32

NEW LETTER

LETTER NAME: *oh*
SOUND IT MAKES: It's a long story!

A few lessons ago, we discussed stressed syllables, syllable duration, and how those factors affect how a vowel is pronounced. And that information will be especially important to remember in this lesson as we study how to make an *o* sound in Russian.

Our new letter for this lesson looks like an English *o*. But just like an English *o*, the Russian letter **о** *(oh)* can have several different sounds. Let's go through each of them.

1. The first sound that we want to mention is the sound that the letter **о** *(oh)* makes when it is on a stressed syllable. This sound is somewhat like the *o* sound in the word *wore*. Notice that when you say the word *wore*, your jaw is very open, and your lips are opening slightly as you pronounce the *o* sound. Another way to think of this sound is to imagine someone from Brooklyn saying the word *coffee*, which would sound something like *KWOHFF-ee*. The *o* sound in that pronunciation of the word *coffee* is

41

what we are referring to. Notice especially that during the pronunciation of this vowel sound, there is a slight opening of the corners of the mouth.

2. This next sound happens when the **о** *(oh)* occurs in the syllable immediately before the stressed syllable in a word. This sound is like the *o* in words such as *dog, frog,* and *log*.

3. And finally, when a Russian **о** *(oh)* comes two syllables before the stress in the word or follows after the stress, it will have a reduced sound. Remember what we said about reduced vowel sounds? When your mouth doesn't have much time, it takes a shortcut and makes a vowel sound into a quick *uh* sound (like the *uh* sound in the first syllable of the word *potato*).

Let's get some practice with the various sounds of the Russian letter **о** *(oh)* by studying a Russian word that has the letter **о** *(oh)* three times—and each time, it's going to sound a little different! In this one word, you'll hear each of the three sounds we just covered above. Here it is—the Russian word for *milk*:

молоко́ *(muh-lah-KOAH)*

In the word **молоко́**, the vowel sound in the first syllable is a reduced vowel sound, which ends up being an *uh* sound. In the second syllable, the vowel sound is like the *o* in *dog, frog,* and *log*. The third and final syllable receives the stress, and so the vowel sound is similar to the *o* in the word *wore* or when someone from Brooklyn says the word *coffee (KWOHFF-ee)*. Put it all together and it sounds something like *muh-lah-KOAH*.

The Russian word for *thank you* shows us an example of the letter **о** *(oh)* when it follows the stress in a word:

спаси́бо *(spah-SEE-buh)*

You can see that the **о** *(oh)* at the end of the word is after the stress, so it is reduced to an *uh* sound.

By the way, this fills in yet another space in our vowel pair chart. It's the hard-indicating version of the vowel that sounds like the *o* in *comb*.

RUSSIAN VOWEL PAIRS	INDICATES HARD CONSONANT	INDICATES SOFT CONSONANT
the *a* in f*a*ther	**а** (ah)	**я** (ya)
the *e* in b*e*d	**э** (eh)	**е** (yeh)
the *e* in f*ee*t		**и** (ee)
the *o* in c*o*mb	**о** (oh)	**ё** (yo)
the *u* in J*u*ne	**у** (ooh)	**ю** (you)

In this lesson, we have tried our best to describe in writing the various *o* sounds in Russian and how to pronounce them correctly. But written descriptions aren't enough! Make sure that you listen carefully to the pronunciation recordings so you can practice pronouncing these sounds with an authentic Russian accent.

LESSON 33

NEW LETTER

LETTER NAME: *ee kratkoyeh* (pronounced *krat-kah-yeh*)
SOUND IT MAKES: adds *ee* sound to another letter

This letter is called *ee kratkoye*. The word *kratkoye* means *short*, so the name translates to *short e*. This letter looks just like **и** *(ee)*, but it has a curly mark over it.

This letter is special because it doesn't operate by itself—instead, it adds a brief *ee* sound before or after a vowel. Therefore, it must come immediately before or after another vowel.

If **й** comes after a vowel, it will add the *ee* sound after the vowel. It's like adding the letter *y* after a vowel in an English word. So if we wanted to spell out the English word *boy* with Russian letters, we could do it like this:

бой

The Russian alphabet doesn't have a single letter that represents the long *i* sound (like the sound of the English word *eye*). So let's say, for example, that there is a word in Russian which was borrowed from English and had a long *i* sound. In Russian they might try to spell it with the Russian letter **а** *(ah)* plus the *ee kratkoye* to make something that sounds like a long *i* sound. For example, if you wanted to spell out the English word *fight*, you could do it like this:

файт

So after the *ah* sound of **а** *(ah)*, then you will pronounce the *ee* sound of **й** *(ee kratkoyeh)* and it sounds something like *FAH-eet*.

When **й** *(ee kratkoyeh)* comes before a vowel, it adds a brief *ee* sound before that vowel. The only vowel you are likely to see following **й** *(ee kratkoyeh)* is the letter

o *(oh)*. Therefore, if we wanted to spell out the English word *yo-yo* with Russian letters, we could do it like this:

йо-йо

So here, you'll start out with the *ee* sound of **й** *(ee kratkoyeh)*, and then say the *oh* sound of **o** *(oh)*. Then repeat! The result sounds something like *ee-oh ee-oh*.

Here is a little chart to help you learn the sounds of a few of the various letter combinations.

COMBINATION	SOUND
эй	*a* in *May*
ай	*i* in *line*
ой	*oy* in *boy*

In the exercises below, watch out for **й** *(ee kratkoyeh)* before or after a vowel. Can you sound out words like *fight*, *yo-yo*, *Amy*, and *boy*?

EXERCISES

1. файт
2. йо-йо
3. Эйми
4. бой
5. той
6. пойнт
7. билив
8. байт
9. изи
10. ойл
11. фойл
12. папая
13. мув
14. пэг
15. Стив
16. бэст
17. плиз
18. елп
19. гис
20. чэст

Answers on page 250.

LESSON 34

NEW LETTER

LETTER NAME: *zheh*
SOUND IT MAKES: the *s* in *pleasure*

Our new letter for this lesson sounds like the *zh* sound you hear in words like *pleasure*, *treasure*, and *vision*. This sound is actually much more common in French than in English.

In the exercises below, we managed to spell out a few words with this sound. Can you find the words *beige*, *massage*, *Jacques*, *espionage*, and *luge*?

EXERCISES

1. бэйж
2. масаж
3. Жак
4. эспионаж
5. луж
6. йо-йо
7. пойнт
8. эгз
9. зу
10. байт
11. билив
12. Эйми
13. ет
14. гэс
15. бой
16. лаг
17. шэф
18. той
19. эг наг
20. папая
21. яц
22. чес
23. шак
24. мют

Answers on page 250.

LESSON 35

THE SOFT SIGN

In the Russian alphabet there is a special character called the *soft sign*. It looks sort of like a lower case *b*. Here it is:

The soft sign does not have a sound of its own. Instead, it affects the consonant right before it, much like the soft-indicating vowels you have learned so far. When you see a soft sign, it means that the preceding consonant will be soft (palatalized) even if there is no soft-indicating vowel to show it. Let's look at some examples of how the soft sign works in actual Russian words.

Here's the Russian word for *corner*. Notice that the last letter of this word is the letter **л** *(el)*.

у́гол

The **л** *(el)* at the end of this word is pronounced with a hard (non-palatalized) *l* sound, so the word sounds something like *OOOH-gull*.

Now, watch what happens when we add the soft sign to the end of this word, right after the **л** *(el)*:

у́голь

With the **л** *(el)* followed by the soft sign, the *l* sound at the end is soft (palatalized). This means that the *l* sound at the end will be pronounced with the tongue raised toward the roof of the mouth. This drastically changes the quality of the *l* sound. (By the way, with the soft sign there at the end, it's a completely different Russian word—the word for a piece of coal!)

Here's a little exercise for you: Take a word that ends with an *l* sound, such as the word *seagull*. First, pronounce it the normal way. Notice that your tongue is probably retracted into the back of your mouth as you pronounce the *l* sound at the end. Now, try to say *seagull* with a Russian soft *l* sound at the end. As you say the *l* sound at the end of the word, raise the middle of your tongue. Can you hear how the position of your tongue changes the sound quality of the *l* sound?

The tongue positions in this exercise will at least help to raise your awareness about the differences between the two words we showed you above. And, as we always say, be sure to listen carefully to the recordings that we have provided. That's really the best way to hear the subtle differences in tone quality that are produced by changes in tongue position.

LESSON 36

SOUNDS WE DON'T HAVE IN ENGLISH

Up to this point we have been spelling out English words with Russian letters. It's sort of a gimmick we made up to help you get started reading the Russian alphabet. It has worked so far because in English we have many of the same (or at least similar) sounds that Russian has.

But there are still a few Russian letters we have not yet taught you. And we can't use these letters to spell out English words because these letters represent sounds that we don't have in English. You see, Russian is a Slavic language, and while English does share some sounds with Slavic languages, there are certain sounds in Russian that you have never made before and will be unfamiliar to you. In fact, this is why St. Cyril and his brother Methodius had to create new characters for their alphabet—because Slavic languages had their own special sounds.

Sooooo…over the next few lessons we will examine the few remaining letters of the Russian alphabet—letters that represent sounds that might be foreign to you. We will try to think of various explanations and gimmicks to help you learn these sounds, but we can't do it all for you—if you want to develop an authentic Russian accent, you are going to have to put in the effort to try to pronounce these unfamiliar sounds correctly. Be ready and willing to open your mouth and practice making new, unfamiliar sounds. Don't be afraid to experiment! Also, learn to listen to the pronunciation recordings carefully, in a detail-oriented manner. Try to hear exactly how the words sound so that you can try to copy those sounds. You must first have an accurate idea of how a word sounds before you can copy it. You can even record yourself to see if you are pronouncing the sounds correctly.

So, as we move into the last few letters of the Russian alphabet, try to think of it as an adventure. Experiment with some new sounds, and don't be afraid to make a mistake or sound silly while you learn!

LESSON 37

THE R SOUND

If you study foreign languages long enough, you will find that there are basically three different ways to pronounce an *r* sound in the various languages.

1. The usual English *r* (like the *urr* sound at the beginning of the word *rabbit*)
2. A rolled Spanish *r* (when your tongue taps lightly against the roof of your mouth)
3. A French *r* (a gurgling sound in the back of the mouth)

In Russian, the kind of *r* sound that is used is #2, a lightly rolled or trilled *r* like the kind used in Spanish. It's not a heavy rolling sound—really just more of a flap or tap of the tip of the tongue against the roof of the mouth.

Below is the Russian letter than makes an *r* sound:

р

The name of the letter is *ehr* and it looks sort of like a lower case *p*. The reason it looks this way is because it is really the Greek letter *rho*, which looks like this:

Back in the time of the ancient Romans, the Greek letter *rho* looked like this:

P

But then the Romans added an extra "leg" to the letter *rho,* and that's why our letter *r* looks the way it does today (in its upper case form, at least).

R

So that's why these letters "r" the way they "r." But all kidding aside, we can't really describe the Russian *r* sound to you with words alone—you need to listen carefully to the audio recordings so you can hear it for yourself.

LESSON 38

NEW LETTER

LETTER NAME: *cha*
SOUND IT MAKES: similar to the letter *h*

This new letter looks just like the letter *x*, but don't confuse it with that letter. The reason it looks like an *x* is because it is really the Greek letter *chi*, which looks like this:

Our new letter for this lesson sounds similar to the pronunciation of the letter *h* in English. With this letter, however, the back of the tongue is raised slightly, making a sort of whooshing sound in the rear of the mouth. Be sure to listen to the audio recordings for this one!

LESSON 39

NEW LETTER

Щ

LETTER NAME: *shsha*
SOUND IT MAKES: like the *sh-sh* in the phrase *fresh sheets*

The name of this letter is *shsha*. It looks just like another letter that you already know—the letter *shah*—except with a little tail hanging from the right side. Let's compare them side by side so you can note the difference in their appearance.

Щ Ш

You might be asking this question: *Why do we have two letters that sound the same? They both make a sh sound, right?* Well, it's not quite that simple. Both letters do make a *sh* sound, but these two sounds are a little different from each other. They each have a slightly different tone quality.

Let's try a little experiment: say the *sh* in *show*. As you sustain that *sh* sound, try moving your tongue around a bit. Move it upward and forward, and close your jaw slightly, listening to the change in sound. Then move your tongue in the opposite direction, retracting your tongue downward and back, opening your jaw slightly. Again, listen to the change in sound. What did you notice?

What we were hoping you noticed is that with your tongue forward and high in your mouth, the *sh* is more of a bright-sounding, higher-pitched sound. And that's the kind of sound that the letter **Щ** *(shsha)* represents. The reason we use the phrase *fresh sheets* to teach you how to pronounce the **Щ** *(shsha)* is that when you start to pronounce the word *sheets* your tongue moves up and to the front of your mouth, right behind your top teeth. This is what produces the higher, brighter *sh* quality.

On the other hand, with your tongue lower and further back, the *sh* sound is more of a dark-sounding, lower-pitched sound. And that's the kind of sound you should make when you pronounce the letter Ш *(shah)*.

Here's a side-by-side comparison of these two letters for study purposes.

shsha	*shah*
Щ	Ш
• tongue high/forward	• tongue low and retracted
• bright sound	• darker sound
• jaw slightly less open	• jaw slightly more open
• higher pitch	• lower pitch
• always soft (palatalized)	• always hard (non-palatalized)

As you can see in the study guide above, the letter Щ *(shsha)* is always soft (palatalized). This means that no matter what letter comes after it, even a hard-indicating vowel, it will always be soft. Furthermore, the letter Ш *(shah)* is always hard. This means that no matter what letter comes after it, even a soft-indicating vowel, it will always be hard.

LESSON 40

NEW LETTER

LETTER NAME: *y*
SOUND IT MAKES: somewhat like the *i* in *ill*

Our new letter for this lesson is a vowel named *y*, but it has several other more outdated names such as *yery*, *yeru*, *ery*, and *eru*. This letter looks sort of like two letters—like a lower case *b* and *l* together, but it's really just one letter.

The sound that this vowel represents does not exist in English, so it will require a bit of explanation. Here's a trick that can help you try to make this sound: say the word *ill* slowly. As you say this word, you should feel your tongue moving up and toward the rear of your mouth. About halfway between the *i* sound and the *l* sound, your tongue will be floating in the center of your mouth, with the sides of your tongue touching your top teeth. When your tongue reaches that spot, try to hold that position and relax your tongue. The sound you make should be a throaty kind of sound that comes from the back of your mouth.

Here is another method to try. Make the sound of the *oo* in the word *boot*, and as you are holding the sound, slowly form your lips into a smile. Pay close attention to what you are feeling and hearing. That is the position you should try to imitate when making this vowel sound. This takes practice!

There is not a very good way to express this sound using English letters. The standard way is to use the letter *y*. We will stick with that standard method when giving pronunciations of Russian words, but we will place the *y* in parentheses to remind you that it is not a true *y* sound.

This lesson is a significant one because Ы *(y)* is the final addition to our vowel pair chart. Behold! The completed chart is below.

RUSSIAN VOWEL PAIRS	INDICATES HARD CONSONANT	INDICATES SOFT CONSONANT
the *a* in f*a*ther	**а** (ah)	**я** (ya)
the *e* in b*e*d	**э** (eh)	**е** (yeh)
the *e* in f*ee*t	**ы** (y)	**и** (ee)
the *o* in c*o*mb	**о** (oh)	**ё** (yo)
the *u* in J*u*ne	**у** (ooh)	**ю** (you)

Hopefully this chart will give you a clear idea of how all the different Russian vowel sounds relate to each other.

Be sure to listen carefully to the audio examples that accompany this lesson—and don't be afraid to experiment with making new and unfamiliar sounds!

LESSON 41

THE HARD SIGN

Our new letter for this lesson is called the *hard sign*, and it is the rarest of all Russian letters. It looks sort of like a lower case *b*, but with a line sticking out from the top. Here it is:

ъ

This hard sign does not have its own sound—in fact, the letter itself is really more of a historical relic than a letter. After the Russian Revolution in 1917, the Soviets introduced spelling reforms in 1918 in order to make Russian spelling more consistent. At that time, the hard sign was used at the ends of words to indicate that the consonant at the end of the word should be pronounced with a hard consonant sound—so it was decided that the hard sign was unnecessary because you could simply assume that the final consonant was hard if there was no soft sign there.

Nowadays, the hard sign is only used in a very few places. For example, you might see it wedged in between the prefix and the root of a word. You should familiarize yourself with this letter so that if you happen to see it, you will recognize it and not confuse it with other similar-looking letters—but you won't need to pronounce it.

LESSON 42

REVIEW

In this review lesson, we would like you to stop for a moment and look back over all you have learned. We hope you'll agree that you've come a long way since lesson 1. You should definitely give yourself a pat on the back, or do something nice for yourself, or at least take a coffee break. But don't rest on your laurels too long, because now that you are familiar with the Russian alphabet, the journey is just beginning. Soon you'll learn some real Russian words, and you'll learn how to construct simple Russian sentences. But before we continue, we would like to review the things that we have taught you so far. These are general concepts and facts that we would like you to remember as we move forward.

1. The Russian alphabet is based upon the Greek alphabet. For this reason, some letters may look familiar to you because the English alphabet is also related to the Greek alphabet.

2. Most of the time, an upper case Russian letter looks the same as its lower case form. In fact, out of the 33 Russian printed letters, 29 of them just use larger and smaller versions for upper and lower case. The other four look different in their upper and lower case forms (**А/а**, **Б/б**, **Е/е**, **Ё/ё**).

3. The roof of your mouth is called the *palate*. Palatalization is when you raise the middle of your tongue up to the roof of your mouth while pronouncing a sound.

4. In Russian, most consonants can be pronounced two ways: hard and soft. A consonant with a hard pronunciation is generally pronounced the same way it would be in English—nothing special or unusual about it. But a consonant with a soft pronunciation is pronounced with palatalization, meaning that you must raise the middle of your tongue to the roof of your mouth while you pronounce the consonant.

5. Palatalization is not something that happens after a consonant. In other words, it does not mean pronouncing a *yi* sound on the next syllable. Instead, palatalization is something you do *during* the pronunciation of a consonant. For example, seeing the word **нет** transliterated as *nyet* might be misleading because it might lead you to believe that the *y* sound happens after the *n* sound is complete—but really they are simultaneous.

6. In Russian, vowels come in pairs. One vowel in each pair indicates that the previous consonant is hard, while the other indicates that the previous consonant is soft. We can use the terms *hard-indicating* and *soft-indicating* to describe them.

7. The sound of a Russian vowel can vary depending on whether it is on a stressed or unstressed syllable. For example, in the word **молоко́** the **о** on the last syllable is part of a stressed syllable, while the other **о** sounds are on unstressed syllables (see lesson 32).

8. Russian is not usually written with markings to show what syllable receives the stress, except in materials such as textbooks and dictionaries. In this book we will use accent marks to show what syllable receives the stress. For example, in the word **маши́на** we will put an accent mark over the second syllable to show you that it sounds like *mah-SHEEN-uh* or *mah-SHIN-uh*.

And as long as we are reviewing things, here is a complete list of the letters of the Russian alphabet in Russian alphabetical order.

THE RUSSIAN ALPHABET

А а *ah*	**К к** *ka*	**Х х** *cha*
Б б *beh*	**Л л** *el*	**Ц ц** *tseh*
В в *veh*	**М м** *em*	**Ч ч** *cheh*
Г г *ghe*	**Н н** *en*	**Ш ш** *shah*
Д д *deh*	**О о** *oh*	**Щ щ** *shsha*
Е е *yeh*	**П п** *peh*	**Ъ ъ** hard sign
Ё ё *yoh*	**Р р** *ehr*	**Ы ы** *y*
Ж ж *zheh*	**С с** *es*	**Ь ь** soft sign
З з *zeh*	**Т т** *te*	**Э э** *eh*
И и *ee*	**У у** *ooh*	**Ю ю** *yu*
Й й *ee kratkoyeh*	**Ф ф** *ef*	**Я я** *ya*

LESSON 43

SUBJECTS AND VERBS

In any sentence, the two most important elements are the subject and the verb. Let's take a moment now to think about subjects and verbs.

A noun is a person, place, or thing. The subject of a sentence is the noun that is doing the action in the sentence. In each of the following examples, the underlined word is the subject of the sentence.

- <u>Matthew</u> kicked the ball.
- <u>Canada</u> is a large country.
- <u>Flowers</u> need sunshine.

Now let's talk about verbs. Verbs are words that tell us what the subject of the sentence is doing. Verbs can be action words such as *dance, shout, walk, talk,* or *write*. Or, they can be verbs of being or existing such as *is, are, was, were,* and *will be*. Verbs of being are also called *linking verbs*. Let's look at those same sentences again, this time underlining the verb in each sentence.

- Matthew <u>kicked</u> the ball.
- Canada <u>is</u> a large country.
- Flowers <u>need</u> sunshine.

For practice, see if you can identify the subject and the verb of each of the following sentences.

EXERCISES

1. Kate walks to school every day.
2. My car is red.
3. My sister likes ice cream.
4. The horse is brown.
5. Harry told me a joke.
6. On Thursdays, Bob plays softball.
7. Mark plays the trumpet.
8. My brother never cleans his room.
9. Julia loves bedtime stories.
10. The students finished their homework.

Answers on page 251.

LESSON 44

LOAN WORDS

So far, we've been giving you English words spelled out with Russian letters. But that was just a temporary trick we used—sort of like training wheels on a bicycle—to help you to get accustomed to the letters of the Russian alphabet. Now that you have a basic working knowledge of the Russian alphabet, the time has come to remove the training wheels and start practicing with real Russian words!

A *loan word* is a word that one language borrows directly from another language. The Russian language has borrowed many words from other languages, including French, German, and English. Although these words start out as words from other languages, when they get absorbed into the Russian language they become real Russian words and take on a distinctively Russian pronunciation.

Over the next few lessons we are going to teach you some loan words that we can use to create simple Russian sentences. Again, these loan words are real Russian words—but they will probably remind you of related English words. When this happens, resist the temptation to pronounce the loan word in an English-sounding way. Instead, listen carefully to each word's pronunciation and try to pronounce them with an authentic Russian pronunciation. The stress might be on a different syllable than the original word, so to help you pronounce the words correctly, we will put an accent mark over the syllable that should receive the stress or emphasis.

Here's our first loan word: the Russian word for *pilot*.

пило́т

The first syllable in the word **пило́т** has the sound of the *ee* in *feet*, which is provided by the letter **и** *(ee)*. The second syllable has an *o* sound—say it with your mouth more open than it would be if you were saying an English *o* sound. As indicated by the accent mark, the emphasis is on the second syllable. Therefore the word **пило́т** sounds something like *pee-LOHT*.

Practice reading and saying this new word because soon we will use it to make simple Russian sentences.

LESSON 45

ARTICLES

As you go further along in your study of Russian, you will need to learn more about grammar—and that means that you will need to learn some new grammatical terms. In this lesson, we would like to teach you a new term: *article*. Articles are words such as *the, a,* and *an*. Articles introduce nouns, like this:

- <u>The</u> man
- <u>The</u> woman
- <u>A</u> chair
- <u>An</u> apple

There are several kinds of articles. Let's examine each one individually.

THE DEFINITE ARTICLE

In English, the word *the* is called the *definite article*. Why? Because when you use it, you are referring to a definite thing. Here's an example:

> Please go into the garage and get <u>the</u> broom.

When you make a statement like this, it is clear that you are referring not to just any broom—instead, you have a specific broom in mind, and you want someone to go and get it! You are referring to a definite thing, therefore *the* is a definite article.

Even when plural, the definite article still works the same way.

> Please go into the garage and get <u>the</u> brooms.

Here, even though you are referring to more than one broom, you still have specific brooms in mind.

THE INDEFINITE ARTICLE

A and *an* are actually the same word, but with one important difference: *a* comes before a word that starts with a consonant and *an* comes before a word that starts with a vowel.

In English, the words *a* and *an* are called *indefinite articles*. Why? Because they don't refer to any specific item. Instead, they just refer to any item that fits the description. Here's an example:

> Please go into the garage and get a broom.

When you make a statement like this, you are not referring to any specific broom. In fact, there may be several brooms in the garage, and you are just asking someone to go and pick one—any broom will do. The thing you are asking for is indefinite, therefore *a* and *an* are indefinite articles.

The word *the* can be used to talk about something singular or something plural. In other words, the word *the* functions as both a singular article and a plural article. But *a* and *an* cannot function as plural articles the way the word *the* can. You cannot say *a brooms* or *an apples*. So, if you are an English speaker, what do you do when you need a plural indefinite article? When we need an indefinite article to be plural, we can express the plural-ness of it by using the word *some*. Here's an example:

> Please go into the garage and get some brooms.

When you make a statement like this, you are not using the word *some* as the opposite of the word *all*, as if to say, "Don't get all of the brooms—make sure you leave a few behind." That's not the point. Instead, the word *some* here is functioning as a plural indefinite article—in other words, a plural form of *a* or *an*. What you mean is that it doesn't matter which brooms the person gets—he or she just needs to get several or a few brooms. Of course, the word *some* isn't really an article, and it's not even required. It's just a common way that English speakers express this kind of thing.

NO ARTICLE

A third kind of "article" is to have no article at all! Some nouns don't need an article to introduce them. This is seen especially with things you can't count or abstract concepts. Here are a few examples of what we mean:

- rice
- generosity
- dirt

You can't count things such as rice or generosity. In other words, you can't have three rice or seven generosity…that doesn't make any sense.

Review this material until it is clear to you, and in the next lesson we will discuss how articles pertain to the Russian language.

LESSON 46

NO ARTICLES IN RUSSIAN

In the last lesson, we told you that nouns can have a definite article *(the)*, an indefinite article *(a, an)*, or no article at all. But in Russian there are no articles—that is, there are no Russian words for *the*, *a*, or *an*. They simply do not exist.

Now you may be wondering at this point…*If Russian doesn't have any articles, why are you spending so much time talking about them?* That's a good question! The reason you need to know about articles is that you will need to use them when you translate from Russian to English. As you read a Russian sentence, the context of the sentence will show you what articles you should put in your English translation.

Here's what we mean. Imagine that you are reading along in a Russian sentence and you see the word **пилóт.** How will you translate it into English?

- pilot
- a pilot
- the pilot

Since there are no articles in Russian, you'll have to decide how you will express it in English—if you'll use a definite article, an indefinite article, or no article at all. In order to make the right choice, you'll need to think about the context. Is the sentence talking about a certain, specific pilot? Or maybe the sentence is referring to pilots in general. The context of the sentence will help you get the "feel" of the word, and whether or not it would have an article in English.

In order to help you understand this concept, we have a little challenge for you. Pretend that the exercises for this lesson are Russian sentences, and you need to translate them into English. We have left a blank in front of certain nouns. Your challenge is to fill in the blank with the correct choice. Choose from one of the following three options:

- the (the definite article)
- a/an (the indefinite article)
- no article

Then, explain why you made that particular choice. Did the context of the sentence suggest something to you? How? Think about the context of the sentence and try to figure out why that particular answer is the best choice. One strategy would be to try each answer and see how it sounds—then try to figure out why it sounded right or wrong.

Here's an example exercise to get you started:

1. When you finish eating, please put your dishes in _____ sink.

Then in the answer key, you'll find a two-part answer—first with the correct choice, and then with the reason why that is the correct choice (in our opinion).

1. ❶ The (the definite article). ❷ Because the speaker is referring to a certain sink (probably the kitchen sink), not just any sink.

EXERCISES

1. Where is _____ book?
2. _____ rice is my favorite food.
3. Whenever I go to school, I always take _____ pencil.
4. Pat doesn't like to mow _____ lawn.
5. I have always wanted to take a trip to _____ Canada.
6. On your way home from work, can you stop off and get me _____ cheeseburger?
7. I usually drink coffee whenever I eat _____ doughnut.
8. I can't talk now because I'm late for _____ school.
9. _____ roof of my house has a leak.
10. This movie is all about _____ superhero.

Answers on page 251.

LESSON 47

NO "AM" IN RUSSIAN

In the last lesson, we learned that the Russian language does not have articles such as *the, a,* or *an.* But those are not the only words that don't exist in Russian—some verbs that we use every day don't exist in Russian either!

In English, we have present tense verbs of being like *am, are,* and *is.* Observe these examples:

- I <u>am</u> the pilot
- You <u>are</u> a student.
- She <u>is</u> the journalist.

But in Russian, those present tense verbs of being don't exist. So if you wanted to say *I am a pilot* in Russian, here is a word-for-word translation of what you would say:

    I pilot.

If you say a sentence like that in Russian, the person you are talking to will know what you mean because of the context in which the conversation is taking place, even though there is no word which corresponds to our word *am.*

Sometimes in Russian there will be a dash where the present tense verb of being would be, like this:

    I — pilot.

So…with no articles, and no present tense verbs of being, it takes fewer words in Russian to say things than it does in English.

LESSON 48

NEW WORD   **Я**

MEANING   *I*

PRONUNCIATION TIP: The word **Я** sounds like *yah*.

A pronoun is a word that takes the place of a noun. Examples of pronouns are words such as *I, you, he, she, it, we,* and *they*.

In this lesson you will learn your first Russian pronoun. You already know that the letter **Я** *(ya)* is a letter of the Russian alphabet. But it's also a pronoun—the Russian word for *I*, as in *I am*. Therefore this letter of the Russian alphabet is both a letter and a word, just like the letter *I* in English.

In English, if we want to say *I am*, it takes two words: the word *I* and then the word *am*. But as we mentioned in the last lesson, there is no Russian word that corresponds to our word *am*. So, let's say that you want to say this in Russian:

> I am a pilot.

Since there is no word for *am* in Russian, and no word for *a* or *an*, you would just put the word **Я**, which means *I*, and the word for *pilot*.

Я пилóт.

This sentence sounds like *ya pee-LOHT*. A word-for-word translation would say *I pilot*. But when you translate it into English, you add in the word *am* and the article *a*, and it all adds up to this: *I am a pilot*.

And, as we mentioned in the last lesson, sometimes they put a dash like this:

Я — пилóт.

Now let's look at the same sentence, but going from Russian to English. Let's say you are reading along and you see the sentence **Я — пилóт**. Without any context, we don't know if the word **пилóт** is supposed to be translated as *a pilot* or *the pilot*. The sentence could be saying *I am a pilot* or *I am the pilot*. So to help you keep in mind that it could be translated both ways, in the answer key, we will put both possibilities. If you are translating an exercise that looks like this...

Я — пилóт.

...in the answer key, here is what the answer for that exercise will look like:

I am the/a pilot.

In other words, whenever there is a Russian exercise that could be translated two ways, we will put both possibilities in the answer key to help you develop a sense or feeling for what the Russian words could be saying.

One last thing before you try the exercises. In English, the pronoun *I* is always capitalized—but in Russian, the pronoun **я** is only capitalized if it is the first word of the sentence.

Got it? Now try to translate these exercises into English.

EXERCISES

1. **я**

2. **Я пилóт.**

3. **Я — пилóт.**

Answers on page 252.

LESSON 49

NEW WORD   **студе́нт**

MEANING   *male student*

Our new word for this lesson is yet another loan word. It sounds similar to our English word *student*, but with two big differences.

First of all, as indicated by the accent mark, the accent is on the second syllable of the word. Also, the letter **д** *(deh)* is soft because it is followed by the vowel **е** *(yeh)* which indicates that the preceding consonant is soft. This means that the **д** *(deh)* is palatalized and you should raise the middle of your tongue when you say it. Therefore the word **студе́нт** sounds something like *stu-D ʸENT*.

The Russian word **студе́нт** means *student*, but more specifically refers to a college or university student. And not only that, **студе́нт** refers particularly to a male student. For female students, we use the same word, but with a special ending that indicates that the student is female. You will learn about this feminine ending later in the book—but for the time being, we will use the word **студе́нт** to make sentences about male students.

EXERCISES

1. **я**
2. **Я студе́нт.**
3. **Я — студе́нт.**
4. **Я пило́т.**
5. **Я — пило́т.**

Answers on page 252.

LESSON 50

NEW WORD **инженéр**

MEANING *engineer*

PRONUNCIATION TIP: The letter **e** *(yeh)* is one of those letters that indicates that the consonant before it is soft. The letter **e** *(yeh)* happens twice in this word, but sounds a bit different each time due to the fact that the second syllable is unstressed, while the last syllable is stressed. Therefore this word sounds something like *een-zhee-N ʸEHR*.

Our new word for this lesson is not someone who drives a train—instead, an **инженéр** can be a mechanical engineer, electrical engineer, etc.

EXERCISES

1. **я**
2. **Я инженéр.**
3. **Я — инженéр.**
4. **Я студéнт.**
5. **Я — студéнт.**
6. **Я пилóт.**
7. **Я — пилóт.**

Answers on page 252.

LESSON 51

NOUN GENDER

In Russian, each noun is classified as having a certain gender. A noun can be either masculine, feminine, or neuter (the word *neuter* means neither masculine nor feminine). Every Russian noun has a gender—not just nouns that refer to people or animals. Even nouns that refer to everyday objects such as boats, tables, mountains, or buildings have gender. So, whenever you learn a new Russian noun, you must make an effort to remember what gender that particular noun is.

Grammatical gender is simply a classification for nouns. This classification (most of the time) is disconnected from the thing that the word represents. For example, the Russian word for *night* is feminine. The Russian word for *day* is masculine. The word for *summer* is neuter—the word *neuter* means *neither*, so a neuter noun is neither masculine nor feminine. Is there something about a day that is somehow masculine? Is the night somehow feminine? No—the grammatical gender of nouns is simply a classification for words—again, it is the word itself that is being classified as masculine, feminine, or neuter, not the thing that the noun means or represents.

That having been said, nouns that refer to people will match the gender that you would expect. For example, the Russian words for *father, brother, grandfather, nephew,* and *uncle* are all grammatically masculine. Likewise, the Russian words for *mother, sister, grandmother, niece,* and *aunt* are all grammatically feminine.

In this book you have seen nouns that are grammatically masculine, but can be used to refer to both men and women. Examples of nouns like this are **пилóт** and **инженéр.** But for other people-words, there is one form of the word that is usually designated for men and then a separate form of the word designated for women. An example of a noun like this would be **студéнт.** A **студéнт** is a male student, and there is a separate word for a female student which we will teach you later in the book. We apologize for making you wait to learn the feminine form, but it's less confusing for you (and us!) if we teach it to you in this order.

LESSON 52

NEW WORD **журнали́ст**

MEANING *journalist*

PRONUNCIATION TIP: The first letter of this word is the letter **Ж** *(zhe)* which has the *zh* kind of sound found in words like *vision* and *pleasure*. Notice also that in the last syllable the letter **и** *(ee)* provides the sound of the *ee* in *feet*. The stress is on the last syllable. Therefore the word **журнали́ст** will sound something like *zhoor-nah-LʸEEST.*

Our new word for this lesson is yet another loan word, this time from French: the Russian word for *journalist*.

This word can refer to a journalist of either gender—however, there is a separate noun with a feminine ending that specifically refers to a female journalist. In the meantime, translate the word **журнали́ст** simply as *journalist*.

EXERCISES

1. **Я**
2. **Я журнали́ст.**
3. **Я — журнали́ст.**
4. **Я инжене́р.**
5. **Я — инжене́р.**
6. **Я студе́нт.**
7. **Я — студе́нт.**
8. **Я пило́т.**
9. **Я — пило́т.**

Answers on page 252.

LESSON 53

NEW WORD   **не**

MEANING   *not*

PRONUNCIATION TIP: The letter **e** *(yeh)* is one of those letters that indicates that the previous consonant is soft, therefore you might expect the word **не** to sound something like *nʸeh*. But because this word is very quick and unstressed, it really sounds something like the English word *knee*.

When you negate a verb, you indicate that the action of the verb is not happening. In English, we use the word *not* to negate a verb.

- I am your brother.
- I am not your brother.

To negate a verb in Russian, we use the word **не** *(nʸee)* which means *not*. Here's a sentence we can practice with:

Я пилóт. *(I am a pilot.)*

To negate this sentence, add in the word **не** right before the word **пилóт** like this:

Я не пилóт. *(I am not a pilot.)*

This sentence sounds like *yah-nʸee-pee-LOHT*. A word-for-word translation would say *I not pilot*. But when we translate it into English, we add in the words *am* and *a*, and we get *I am not a pilot*.

If there is a dash in place of the verb of being, the dash will come before the word **не**, like this:

Я — не пилóт. *(I am not a pilot.)*

EXERCISES

1. Я пило́т.
2. Я не пило́т.
3. Я — не пило́т
4. Я — студе́нт.
5. Я — не студе́нт.
6. Я инжене́р.
7. Я — не инжене́р.
8. Я журнали́ст.
9. Я не журнали́ст.
10. Я — не журнали́ст.

Answers on page 252.

LESSON 54

NEW WORD **дипломáт**

MEANING *diplomat*

PRONUNCIATION TIP: The letter **и** *(ee)* is one of those letters that indicates that the previous consonant is soft (palatalized). The **о** *(oh)* comes before the stressed syllable, so it sounds like the *a* in *father*. Therefore this word sounds like *dʸeep-lah-MAHT*.

Our new word for this lesson is yet another loan word, this time from French (although we have the word *diplomat* in English, too).

EXERCISES

1. **Я дипломáт.**
2. **Я не дипломáт.**
3. **Я — не журналíст.**
4. **Я не журналíст.**
5. **Я журналíст.**
6. **Я инженéр.**
7. **Я не инженéр.**
8. **Я — студéнт.**
9. **Я — не студéнт.**
10. **Я пилóт.**

Answers on page 252.

LESSON 55

NEW WORD **бизнесме́н**

MEANING *businessperson*

PRONUNCIATION TIP: The letters **и** *(ee)* and **е** *(yeh)* are soft-indicating vowels. This means that the letters **б** *(beh)*, **н** *(en)*, and **м** *(em)* in this word are soft. Therefore this word sounds like *bʸeez-nʸees-Mʸ EN*.

This loan word is related to our English word *businessman*—nevertheless, it can refer to either men or women, so we translate it as *businessperson*.

EXERCISES

1. **Я бизнесме́н.**
2. **Я — не бизнесме́н.**
3. **Я — бизнесме́н.**
4. **Я дипломáт.**
5. **Я не дипломáт.**
6. **Я журнали́ст.**
7. **Я не журнали́ст.**
8. **Я — не инжене́р.**
9. **Я студе́нт.**
10. **Я не пило́т.**

Answers on page 252.

LESSON 56

NEW WORD **и**

MEANING *and*

PRONUNCIATION TIP: This word sounds like the *ee* in *feed*.

You already know the letter **и** *(ee)* just as a letter. But in Russian, this letter is also a word that means *and*. Use it just like you would use the word *and* in English, like this:

Я — пилóт и журналúст. *(I am a pilot and a journalist.)*

1. **Я бизнесмéн и дипломáт.**
2. **Я не бизнесмéн.**
3. **Я — дипломáт и пилóт.**
4. **Я не дипломáт.**
5. **Я студéнт и инженéр.**
6. **Я — не инженéр.**
7. **Я — пилóт и бизнесмéн.**
8. **Я не пилóт.**
9. **Я — дипломáт и бизнесмéн.**
10. **Я — не бизнесмéн.**

Answers on page 253.

LESSON 57

NEW WORD **ты**

MEANING *you*

PRONUNCIATION TIP: This word consists of two characters: the letter **т** *(teh)* and the letter **ы** *(y)*. Remember that **ы** *(y)* makes a sort of throaty sound. When we spell out Russian pronunciations with English letters, we will represent this sound as a letter *y* in parentheses, like this: *(y)*. You can refer back to lesson 40 to review how to pronounce it. The pronunciation is *t(y)*. When you listen to the recording, you may notice that the **т** *(teh)* does not have as much "pop" to it as our English *t*, and that is even more the case when it is combined with the letter **ы** *(y)*. When pronouncing the English *t*, we generally place the tip of the tongue against the ridge above the teeth. The Russian pronunciation, however, involves more surface area of the tongue, and it is the top of the tongue that makes contact against the ridge above the teeth. This softens the impact of the *t* sound and prepares the mouth for the upcoming vowel. You really need to listen to the recordings to get a good idea of how to pronounce this word.

So far, you know only one pronoun: the word **я**, which means *I*. But now, it's time to start learning other pronouns such as *you, he, she, it, we,* and *they*. In this lesson, you'll start practicing with the Russian word for *you*, which is **ты**.

The pronoun **ты** is singular, meaning that you use it when speaking to only one person. You can use **ты** in a sentence the same way you would use **я**, like this:

Ты — пилóт. *(You are a pilot.)*

Just as with the word *am*, there is no word in Russian for *are*. So a word-for-word translation would say *You pilot*. But when we translate it into English we add in the words *are* and *a*, and we get *You are a pilot*. Of course, it could also be translated as *You are the pilot*.

EXERCISES

1. ты

2. Ты — пилóт.

3. Ты не — журналист.

4. Ты не диплома́т.

5. Ты студе́нт и инжене́р.

6. Ты не студе́нт.

7. Я инжене́р и пило́т.

8. Я — бизнесме́н и студе́нт.

9. Я не студе́нт.

10. Я — диплома́т.

Answers on page 253.

LESSON 58

NEW WORD **он**

MEANING *he*

PRONUNCIATION TIP: This word sounds something like if you said *o-wun* very quickly, but with your mouth more open. Be sure to listen to the recordings!

The word **он** is a masculine pronoun that means *he*. Here's an example of how you could use it in a sentence:

Он — студе́нт. *(He is a student.)*

Later in your Russian studies you will learn that our new word for this lesson can be translated into English as *it* when referring to an inanimate object that happens to be grammatically masculine. But for our purposes here, we are just using it to mean *he*.

EXERCISES

1. он
2. Он не журналист.
3. Он — пилот и инженер.
4. Он дипломат.
5. Ты бизнесмен и инженер.
6. Ты не бизнесмен.
7. Ты инженер и пилот.
8. Ты пилот и студент.
9. Я инженер.
10. Я — не студент.

Answers on page 253.

LESSON 59

NEW WORDS **она́**

MEANING *she*

PRONUNCIATION TIP: The accent is on the second syllable. Since the **о** *(oh)* at the beginning of **она́** falls on an unstressed syllable, it sounds like the *a* in *father*. Therefore **она́** sounds something like *ah-NAH*.

The word **она́** is a feminine pronoun that means *she*. Here's an example of how you could use it in a sentence:

- **Она́ — пило́т.** *(She is a pilot.)*
- **Она́ — инжене́р.** *(She is an engineer.)*

Remember that the word **студе́нт** is generally used for males, so it wouldn't typically be used with **она́**. But later in the book we will teach you the grammatically feminine form of **студе́нт** that means *female student*.

Later in your Russian studies you will learn that our new word for this lesson can be translated into English as *it* when referring to an inanimate object that happens to be grammatically feminine. But for our purposes here, we are just using it to mean *she*.

EXERCISES

1. **она́**
2. **Она́ пило́т и инжене́р.**
3. **Она́ — не пило́т.**
4. **Он журнали́ст.**
5. **Он диплома́т и бизнесме́н.**
6. **Он не инжене́р.**

7. Ты — не журналист.

8. Ты пилот и студент.

9. Ты — не бизнесмен.

10. Я инженер.

Answers on page 253.

LESSON 60

SINGULAR AND PLURAL

Singular means there is one of something.

Plural means there is more than one of something.

Just for practice, try to figure out if the underlined word in each sentence is singular or plural.

EXERCISES

1. I have three <u>cats</u>.
2. Hand me that <u>book</u>, please.
3. I saw a <u>deer</u> in the woods.
4. I want to catch a <u>fish</u>.
5. There are many <u>cars</u> on the road today.
6. I need a new <u>pair</u> of pants.
7. The <u>deer</u> are eating all of my plants!
8. We don't have any more <u>cookies</u>.
9. The <u>fish</u> are in the fishbowl.
10. We painted the wrong <u>house</u>.

Answers on page 253.

LESSON 61

PLURAL NOUNS

In English we can make a noun plural by changing the ending of the word, usually by adding the letter *s* like this:

book ⟶ books

In Russian we can also make nouns plural by changing the ending—but it's not nearly as simple as it is in English. Instead of just one ending to remember, there are…well, it's a long story, so let's take it one step at a time.

For the nouns you know so far, we will add the letter **ы** *(y)* to make them plural. Adding this letter to the end of a word will add our *(y)* sound at the end. Let's practice making nouns plural by adding **ы** *(y)* to the end of the word **пило́т.**

пило́т ⟶ пило́ты

With **ы** *(y)* at the end, **пило́ты** sounds something like *pee-LOHT-(y)*.

Now let's make **студе́нт** plural:

студе́нт ⟶ студе́нты

With the letter **ы** *(y)* at the end, **студе́нты** sounds like *stoo-D ʸENT-(y)*.

For all the nouns you know so far, we will add this ending to make them plural. In the exercises below, we have given you the plural form of each noun. See if you can correctly translate them into English.

EXERCISES

1. **пило́ты**
2. **студе́нты**
3. **инжене́ры**
4. **журнали́сты**
5. **дипломаты**
6. **бизнесме́ны**

Answers on page 254.

LESSON 62

NEW WORD **МЫ**

MEANING *we*

PRONUNCIATION TIP: This word is pronounced *m(y)*. Again, the *(y)* sound takes practice, so keep using the strategies we recommended when we first introduced **Ы** *(y)*. Make sure your tongue is pushed back when you pronounce it, and make sure you keep listening to the recordings and imitating what you hear! If what you produce sounds like the word *me*, keep trying. You might hear a hint of a *w* sound when you pronounce it, but if it sounds like *mwee* then that's too much.

In this lesson you are learning your first plural pronoun: the word **мы** which means *we*.

Мы is a plural pronoun, so if you want to make a sentence with it, you will need to put a plural noun with it, like this:

Мы — пило́ты. *(We are pilots.)*

EXERCISES

1. мы
2. Мы не диплома́ты.
3. Мы инжене́ры и студе́нты.
4. Мы — не бизнесме́ны.
5. Мы журнали́сты.
6. Она́ — не пило́т.
7. Она́ инжене́р и пило́т.
8. Он студе́нт и журнали́ст.

9. Ты пило́т и студе́нт.

10. Я инжене́р.

Answers on page 254.

LESSON 63

NEW WORD   **вы**

MEANING   *you (plural)*

PRONUNCIATION TIP: Here is yet another word that ends in **ы** *(y)*. The pronunciation is *v(y)*. The practice you did with the word **мы** in the previous lesson will help with this one as well. And remember that you can always go back to lesson 40 to review this unusual sound! You might hear a hint of a *w* sound when you pronounce it, but if it sounds like *vwee* then that's too much.

You already know that **ты** means *you*. We use **ты** when speaking to one person. **Вы** also means *you*, but with one important difference: **вы** is plural. The English word *you* can refer to one person or more than one person. But other languages such as Russian, Spanish, French, and German all have a separate word for singular *you* and for plural *you*.

Sometimes English speakers use expressions such as *you all, you guys,* or *you people* to try to make it clear that we are talking to more than one person. In the southeastern United States, we often use the contraction *y'all* to address more than one person (never just one). *Y'all* is simply a contraction of the words *you* and *all*. *Y'all* rhymes with *hall, ball,* and *fall*. So in the answer key, **вы** will be translated as *y'all* to help you distinguish plural *you* from singular *you*. If you are from the southeastern United States, using this word will be easy for you. If not, *y'all* will get used to it after using it a few times. In any case, just try to have fun with it.

Later in the book we will learn how to use this pronoun to speak in a more formal way—but for now, just use it the way we have shown you here.

Here's an example sentence with **вы.**

Вы — пило́ты. *(Y'all are pilots.)*

EXERCISES

1. **вы**
2. **Вы — не дипломáты.**
3. **Вы пилóты.**
4. **Мы инженéры.**
5. **Мы дипломáты и бизнесмéны.**
6. **Онá инженéр и пилóт.**
7. **Онá инженéр.**
8. **Он пилóт и студéнт.**
9. **Ты — не дипломáт.**
10. **Я — не бизнесмéн.**

Answers on page 254.

LESSON 64

NEW WORD **они́**

MEANING *they*

PRONUNCIATION TIP: Sounds something like *ah-NʸEE*.

This word is similar to **она́** *(she)* because only one letter is different—so don't mix them up!

Here's an example sentence with **они́**:

Они́ — дипломáты. *(They are diplomats.)*

EXERCISES

1. они́
2. Они́ не пило́ты.
3. Они́ диплома́ты и бизнесме́ны.
4. Вы студе́нты.
5. Вы не бизнесме́ны.
6. Мы инжене́ры и студе́нты.
7. Она́ инжене́р и пило́т.
8. Он не диплома́т.
9. Ты пило́т и студе́нт.
10. Я — бизнесме́н и студе́нт.

Answers on page 254.

LESSON 65

PERSON

Pronouns and verbs can be in the first person, second person, or third person. This characteristic tells us about the viewpoint or aspect from which the action is being viewed.

- Pronouns and verbs that refer to *I* or *we* are first person (the person who is speaking).

- Pronouns and verbs that refer to *you*, either singular or plural, are second person (the person or people to whom the speaker is speaking). In this book we will use *y'all* for the second person plural to help distinguish it from the second person singular.

- Pronouns and verbs that refer to *he, she, it,* or *they* are third person (the person, thing, people, or things being spoken about).

The following chart should help illustrate this concept:

	SINGULAR	PLURAL
FIRST PERSON	I	we
SECOND PERSON	you	you ← y'all
THIRD PERSON	he, she, it	they

If we put all the Russian pronouns you know in a chart like the one above, it looks like this:

	Singular	Plural
First Person	я	мы
Second Person	ты	вы
Third Person	он/она́	они́

At this point you need to memorize these pronouns and practice saying them until you can say them confidently.

In the exercises below, we have a triple challenge for you. First, determine what the subject of each sentence is. Then, determine if the subject is first person, second person, or third person. Finally, determine whether the subject is singular or plural.

EXERCISES

1. I am hungry.
2. You are a nice person.
3. She is very smart.
4. We are going to the park.
5. Y'all have a beautiful home.
6. They eat lunch at Aunt Martha's house every Sunday.
7. He is a tennis player.
8. It is a history book.
9. Y'all really know how to throw a party.
10. The flowers in your garden are pretty.

Answers on page 254.

LESSON 66

DECLENSIONS

By now, you have learned a few Russian nouns and lots of useful pronouns. You're off to a good start—but now it's time to go into more detail about the grammar of the Russian language so you can start to make more complicated sentences. In Russian, nouns are a big deal—and it's important to understand how they work.

The next big, important thing that we need to teach you is this: A Russian noun can have many different endings. These endings change depending on what a particular noun is doing in a sentence. For example, if a noun is possessing something, it will have a certain possessive ending. If a noun is receiving something, it will have yet another certain ending. In other words, the ending of a Russian noun indicates what role that noun is playing in the sentence.

But these endings aren't random—each noun conforms to a distinct pattern of endings. And these patterns of noun endings are called *declensions* (pronounced *deh-KLEN-shuns*). In the Russian language, there are three declensions—three different patterns of endings that a noun can have. There are different ways to refer to them, but in this book, just for simplicity, we will refer to them as the *first declension*, *second declension*, and *third declension*.

The first declension is a pattern of endings that is used mostly for feminine nouns. The second declension is a pattern of endings mostly for masculine and neuter nouns. All the nouns you know so far, such as **студе́нт** and **диплома́т** use the endings of the second declension. The third declension includes feminine nouns that have different endings than the first declension nouns. Here's a chart that shows the general characteristics of each noun declension.

RUSSIAN NOUN DECLENSIONS		
FIRST DECLENSION	SECOND DECLENSION	THIRD DECLENSION
• generally feminine • nouns end in **а** (ah) or **я** (yah)	• masculine or neuter • masculine nouns generally end in a hard consonant or **й** • neuter nouns end in **о** (oh) or **е** (yeh)	• only feminine • nouns end in **ь** (soft sign) or **я** (yah)

Every Russian noun will belong to one of these three declensions—so whenever you learn a new Russian noun, you need to remember what declension it belongs to. That way, you'll know what endings go along with that particular noun. In this book, we will move slowly and teach you noun endings one at a time.

And, as we said before, the nouns you currently know are all part of the second declension. We gave you these nouns mainly for practice—just to get you started reading simple sentences. But from this point forward, we will no longer be working with the masculine nouns of the second declension. Instead, from now on, we will be working only with feminine nouns from the first declension. The reason for this is that we, the authors, think this is the best way to move you forward in your study of the Russian language. The idea here is that once you have mastered the first declension and all the concepts that go with it, it will be much easier for you to learn the second and third declensions because you will already understand what a declension is and how the whole system works.

So…stick with us, and soon you will be learning all about the first declension. In Russian, the words for *car*, *moon*, and *newspaper* are all feminine nouns of the first declension, so we will start our study of the first declension with these nouns. Later, you will learn people-related nouns (feminine, of course) such as *girl*, *woman*, and *grandmother*.

LESSON 67

NEW WORD   **маши́на**

MEANING   *car*

PRONUNCIATION TIP: Remember that the letter **ш** *(shah)* is always hard and is not affected by soft-indicating vowels. *Shah* has a low-pitched, dark *sh* sound that is produced by retracting the tongue and opening the jaw. This tongue position will affect the sound of the letter **и** *(ee)* that comes immediately after it, causing this word to sound something like *mah-SHEEN-ah* or *mah-SHIN-ah*.

In the last lesson, we explained that for the remainder of the book, the only declension that we will study is the first declension. With that in mind, here is your very first noun from the first declension: the Russian word for *car*.

The singular form of this word is **маши́на** with **-а** *(ah)* as its ending. In order to make it plural, we will replace that ending with **-ы** *(y)* like this:

    маши́на ⟶ **маши́ны**

The **-ы** ending adds the *(y)* sound to the end of the word, therefore **маши́ны** sounds something like *ma-SHIN-(y)*.

In the exercises below, try to translate and correctly pronounce each word.

EXERCISES

  1. маши́на

  2. маши́ны

Answers on page 254.

LESSON 68

NOUN STEMS AND ENDINGS

In the last lesson, you learned that in order to make the word **маши́на** plural, we had to change the ending. In this lesson, we would like to take a bit of time to explain more about noun endings and how they work.

The first thing to know is that a noun has something called a *stem*. The stem is the base of the word, and it always stays the same. Here is the stem of the noun **маши́на**:

маши́н-

Once you know what the stem of a noun is, you can add the various endings to it. Right now, you know two endings:

- **-а**
- **-ы**

So, if you have the stem…

маши́н-

…you can add the endings to it, like this:

маши́н + а = маши́на

Or, like this to make it plural:

маши́н + ы = маши́ны

Not every Russian noun will work this way. There are some special situations in which certain letters will change or go away before the ending of a noun. But for right now, the concept of noun stems and noun endings is an important thing for you to know as you learn nouns of the first declension.

LESSON 69

DIRECT OBJECTS

A direct object is a noun that is the target of the action being performed by the subject of the sentence. Here is an example:

> Harold plays the drums.

In this sentence, the word *drums* is the direct object. Here is another example:

> Helen ate the orange.

In this sentence, the word *orange* is the direct object. See if you can find the direct object in each of the exercises below:

EXERCISES

1. Mr. Jones bought a newspaper.
2. I will see a movie tomorrow.
3. Harry is playing the trombone.
4. On Saturday, we will play baseball.
5. James caught a fish.
6. They accidentally broke the radio.
7. Y'all painted the wrong building.
8. Yesterday we listened to a long speech.
9. Mr. Underwood lost his wallet.
10. Geraldine saw a deer in the woods.

Answers on page 255.

LESSON 70

THE PREDICATE NOMINATIVE

In the last lesson, you learned that a direct object is the target of the action. For example, in the following sentence the word *dog* is the direct object.

    Fred chased the dog.

But what if the verb is not an action verb? What if the verb is a verb of being or existing, as in this example:

    Fred is a dog.

In that sentence, the word *dog* is not a direct object. Why? Because only an action verb can generate a direct object. The verb in that sentence is the word *is*, which is a verb of being. When you use a verb of being to make a "this is that" kind of sentence, the "that" word is not a direct object—instead, it is called a *predicate nominative*. Therefore in the sentence above, the word *dog* is a predicate nominative. Many of the Russian exercises that you have translated so far in this book have included predicate nominatives.

In each of the following exercises the word *dog* is either a direct object or a predicate nominative. See if you can figure out which one it is.

EXERCISES

1. Fluffy is our dog.
2. The cat chased the dog.
3. We saw the dog.
4. Did you feed the dog?
5. The kids are all petting the dog.
6. A golden retriever is a dog.
7. Yesterday we bathed the dog.
8. The vet examined the dog.
9. Rex was our dog.
10. My best friend is a dog.

Answers on page 255.

LESSON 71

DIRECT OBJECTS (THIS TIME IN RUSSIAN)

In Russian, a noun can have many different endings. These endings indicate what function a noun is performing in a sentence. In this lesson you will learn the ending for when a noun is a direct object.

When **маши́на** is the direct object in a sentence, the ending changes to **-у**. Let's see how that ending gets added to the stem. Here is the stem:

маши́н-

Now let's take the ending **-у** and add it to the stem:

маши́н + у = маши́ну

Now we have **маши́ну.** The letter **у** sounds like the *oo* in *boot*, so **маши́ну** sounds something like *mah-SHIN-ooh*.

Let's work with some examples that show the different forms of **маши́на** and how they would be used as a subject, direct object, or predicate nominative.

SUBJECT

In this first example, the car is the subject of the sentence:

The **маши́на** is driving down the street.

In that sentence, the car is the subject of the sentence, so it retains its normal form, which is **маши́на**.

DIRECT OBJECT

In this example, the car is the direct object.

I saw a **маши́ну**.

Since the car is the direct object, the ending changed to **-у** to make **маши́ну**.

PREDICATE NOMINATIVE

In this example, the car is a predicate nominative.

>The vehicle in the garage is a **маши́на**.

In that sentence, the word *vehicle* is the subject of the sentence. The word *is* is the verb, which is a verb of being. The car is a predicate nominative so it retains its normal form, which is **маши́на**. It is not a direct object.

In the exercises below, fill in the blank with either **маши́на** or the direct object form **маши́ну**. Then, give the reason for your choice. Choose from among the following three reasons:

- Because it is the subject of the sentence
- Because it is the direct object of the sentence
- Because it is a predicate nominative

Write your answers in your notebook or on a separate sheet of paper.

EXERCISES

1. Yesterday, I saw a _____ speeding down the highway.
2. A Ferrari is a _____ .
3. A _____ is blocking the road.
4. I rented a _____ for our trip.
5. The _____ rolled down the hill.
6. The _____ has a flat tire.
7. I watched the _____ while the mechanic fixed it.
8. My Christmas gift is a new _____ .
9. My brother drove the _____ .
10. The best invention ever is the _____ .

Answers on page 255.

LESSON 72

NEW WORD **я ви́жу**

MEANING *I see*

PRONUNCIATION TIP: Notice that the letter **в** *(veh)* sounds like a *v*, and that the accent is on the first syllable. Also the letter **и** indicates that the **в** is palatalized. Therefore **ви́жу** sounds like *V^yEE-zhoo*.

The word **ви́жу** is our first action verb in Russian, and it means *I see*. This means that we now know a Russian verb that can take a direct object.

We are presenting this new verb to you as **я ви́жу**, with both the pronoun **я** and the verb **ви́жу**. We will discuss this a bit more a few lessons from now, but for now you should keep in mind that the word **ви́жу** means *I see* even without the pronoun **я**. Even though the pronoun **я** is not required to say *I see*, since you are a beginner we will include it for simplicity and ease of learning.

You may have noticed that this verb sounds somewhat like our English word *vision*. That is no coincidence—they are similar because they are distant cousins. Our English word *vision* is related to the Latin verb **video** which means *I see*, and also to the Latin noun **visio** which means *sight* or *vision*.

In the last lesson, we learned that if **маши́на** is a direct object, the ending changes to **-у** and becomes **маши́ну**. Here's an example of how this works:

Я ви́жу маши́ну. *(I see the/a car.)*

In that particular sentence, the car was the direct object, so we used the direct object form of the word, which is **маши́ну**.

If you want to negate the verb, put the word **не** before the verb, like this:

Я не ви́жу маши́ну. *(I do not see the/a car.)*

EXERCISES

1. я
2. Я ви́жу.
3. Я не ви́жу.
4. маши́на
5. маши́ны
6. Я ви́жу маши́ну.
7. Я не ви́жу маши́ну.
8. Я — не маши́на.

Answers on page 255.

LESSON 73

NEW WORD   **Луна́**

MEANING   *moon*

PRONUNCIATION TIP: The accent is on the second syllable, so **Луна́** sounds like *loo-NAH*.

The ancient Roman word for *moon* was the Latin word **luna**. As Latin slowly evolved into Spanish in Spain, that word survived and is now the Spanish word for *moon*. That Latin word is also where we get our English word *lunar* which means *moon-related*. When the moon goes through its various phases, we call that the lunar cycle, and when a spaceship lands on the moon, it's called a lunar landing.

In Russian, the word **Луна́** only refers to Earth's moon—notice that it is capitalized because this word is treated as the moon's name (like Fred, Barbara, or Natasha). If you want to talk about the moons of some other planet such as Jupiter, the word you would use is **спу́тник** (pronounced *SPOOT-nʸeek*). You may be familiar with this word already in its English form because the word *sputnik* is famous in the history of space exploration.

A satellite, by definition, is something that orbits around a larger object. For this reason, the Russian word **спу́тник** refers both to natural objects that orbit, like moons, and man-made objects like a mechanical satellite. That's why in 1957 when the Soviet Union launched the first satellite into space, they called it *Sputnik 1*.

The stem of **Луна́** is **Лун-**, so if you want to create the different forms of this noun, take the stem and add the various endings like this:

- **Лун** + **а** = **Луна́**
- **Лун** + **ы** = **Луны́**
- **Лун** + **у** = **Луну́**

EXERCISES

1. Луна́
2. Я ви́жу.
3. Я не ви́жу.
4. Я ви́жу Луну́.
5. Я не ви́жу Луну́.
6. маши́на
7. маши́ны
8. Я ви́жу маши́ну.
9. Я не ви́жу маши́ну.
10. Я — не маши́на.

Answers on page 255.

LESSON 74

DEMONSTRATIVES

In this lesson we will take a moment to examine the words *this, that, these,* and *those*. In grammatical terms, these words are known as demonstratives (pronounced *duh-MAHN-stra-tivz*). We call them demonstratives because we use them in conversation to verbally point out (that is, demonstrate) the people or things that we are referring to. There are two ways to use demonstratives, so let's take a look at each of them.

One way to use a demonstrative is as an adjective. When you use a demonstrative in this way, it is called a *demonstrative adjective*. In each example sentence below, notice that the demonstrative adjective (underlined) is describing a noun.

- <u>This</u> tree is huge.
- I never go to <u>that</u> restaurant.
- I don't like <u>these</u> cookies.
- <u>Those</u> books are dusty.

But demonstratives don't always have to describe a noun. A demonstrative can stand on its own, representing something or someone just as a pronoun would. When demonstratives are used in this way, they are called *demonstrative pronouns*. In each example sentence below, notice that a demonstrative pronoun (underlined) is representing something on its own, without describing a noun.

- <u>This</u> is my car.
- I didn't see <u>that</u>.
- <u>These</u> are too big.
- We rarely ever use <u>those</u>.

When you understand this concept, turn the page and we will begin working with demonstratives in Russian.

LESSON 75

NEW WORD   **э́то**

MEANING   *this is, that is, these are, those are*

PRONUNCIATION TIP: The **э** *(eh)* at the beginning of this word sounds like the *e* in *bed*, and the **о** *(oh)* is reduced because the accent is on the first syllable. Therefore **э́то** sounds roughly like *EH-tuh*.

Our new word for this lesson, **э́то**, is a flexible, all-purpose kind of Russian demonstrative that can be used in different ways to point things out in conversation. It's a long story, but in this book we will teach you how to use it as a demonstrative pronoun. When you use **э́то** in this way, there is an understood verb of being along with it, so **э́то** can mean several different things depending on the context: *this is, these are, that is,* or *those are*.

Here are some example sentences in which **э́то** is working as a demonstrative pronoun. As usual, there may or may not be a dash there to represent the verb of being.

- **Э́то — Светла́на.** *(This is Svetlana.)*
- **Э́то маши́ны.** *(These are cars.)*
- **Э́то Кла́ра.** *(That is Clara.)*
- **Э́то — маши́ны.** *(Those are cars.)*

Again, to provide an exact translation of **э́то** you'll need some context. Since the exercises in this book are short and don't have much context, in the answer key we will translate **э́то** with *This is/that is* if the sentence is referring to something singular and *These are/those are* if it is referring to more than one item.

EXERCISES

1. **Э́то — маши́на.**
2. **Э́то — маши́ны.**

3. Э́то не маши́на.
4. Э́то маши́ны.
5. Я не ви́жу Луну́.
6. маши́на
7. маши́ны
8. Я ви́жу маши́ну.
9. Э́то Луна́.
10. Э́то не Луна́.

Answers on page 255.

LESSON 76

NEW WORD **газе́та**

MEANING *newspaper*

PRONUNCIATION TIP: The letter **e** *(yeh)* indicates that the previous consonant is soft, so this word sounds like *ga-ZʸET-uh*.

Long ago, in the city of Venice, Italy, the price of a newspaper was one coin, which was called a *gazeta*. For this reason the word *gazeta* became the word for the newspaper itself. This Italian word was borrowed into French, and from there into Russian as the word **газе́та**.

The plural form of **газе́та** is **газе́ты**, and the direct object form is **газе́ту**.

EXERCISES

1. **газе́та**
2. **газе́ты**
3. **Я ви́жу газе́ту.**
4. **Э́то — газе́та.**
5. **Э́то газе́ты.**
6. **Э́то Луна́.**
7. **Я не ви́жу Луну́.**
8. **Э́то маши́на.**
9. **Э́то не маши́ны.**
10. **Я ви́жу маши́ну.**

Answers on page 256.

LESSON 77

PLURAL DIRECT OBJECTS

When nouns such as **газе́та**, **Луна́**, and **маши́на** become direct objects, the ending changes to **-у**. But what happens if the direct object is plural? What ending will it have?

With all the nouns we are presently working with, the plural form of the direct object will be the same as the regular plural form. Therefore, for the noun **маши́на**, the direct object plural form will be **маши́ны**.

Here's an example of a sentence with a plural direct object:

Я ви́жу маши́ны. *(I see (the) cars.)*

EXERCISES

1. **Я не ви́жу маши́ну.**
2. **Я ви́жу маши́ны.**
3. **Э́то не маши́на.**
4. **Э́то маши́ны.**
5. **Я ви́жу газе́ту.**
6. **Я ви́жу газе́ты.**
7. **Я не ви́жу Луну́.**
8. **Э́то не маши́ны.**
9. **Э́то газе́та.**
10. **Я ви́жу Луну́.**

Answers on page 256.

LESSON 78

NEW WORD **у́лица**

MEANING *street*

PRONUNCIATION TIP: You haven't seen the letter **ц** *(tseh)* in a long time. It sounds like the *ts* in *hits*. The stress is on the first syllable, so it sounds like *OOH-lee-tsah*.

The plural form of **у́лица** is **у́лицы**, and the direct object form is **у́лицу**. The plural direct object form is also **у́лицы**.

EXERCISES

1. **Э́то у́лицы.**
2. **Я ви́жу у́лицы.**
3. **Я ви́жу маши́ну и у́лицу.**
4. **Я не ви́жу газе́ту.**
5. **Я ви́жу газе́ты.**
6. **Я ви́жу Луну́.**
7. **Я — не маши́на.**
8. **Э́то газе́ты.**
9. **Э́то Луна́.**
10. **Я не ви́жу у́лицу.**

Answers on page 256.

LESSON 79

NEW WORD   ТЫ ВИ́ДИШЬ

MEANING   *you see*

PRONUNCIATION TIP: You may have noticed that this word has a soft sign (**ь**) at the end. In fact, this is the first time you have seen the soft sign in an actual Russian word. However, the soft sign is actually a historical leftover in this verb form, and it does not have any effect on the pronunciation because the letter **Ш** *(shah)* is always hard. Therefore, the **Ш** *(shah)* remains unchanged, and **ви́дишь** sounds something like *VEE-d^yeesh*.

For a long time you have been only working with the verb **ви́жу**, which is first person singular. But now, it's time for you to learn the other forms of this verb—forms you can use to say things like *you see, he sees, she sees, we see*, etc. Therefore, in this lesson you will learn the second person singular form, which will allow you to say *you see*.

The second person singular form of **ви́жу** is the word **ви́дишь**. This word is special because, as mentioned above, it is the first Russian word you have learned that has the soft sign in it.

Over the next few lessons, you will gradually learn all the present tense forms of **я ви́жу**. As we learn each new form one at a time, we will gradually fill in the chart which you see below, and it will help you keep track of your progress.

	SINGULAR	PLURAL
FIRST PERSON	я ви́жу	
SECOND PERSON	ты ви́дишь	
THIRD PERSON		

Here's an example sentence that uses our new verb for this lesson.

Ты ви́дишь маши́ну. *(You see the car.)*

EXERCISES

1. **Ты ви́дишь у́лицу.**
2. **Ты не ви́дишь у́лицы.**
3. **Ты ви́дишь газе́ты.**
4. **Ты ви́дишь Луну́.**
5. **Ты не ви́дишь у́лицу.**
6. **Я ви́жу маши́ну.**
7. **Я ви́жу у́лицу и маши́ны.**
8. **Э́то газе́та.**
9. **Э́то не маши́ны.**
10. **Э́то у́лицы.**

Answers on page 256.

LESSON 80

NEW WORD **он/она́ ви́дит**

MEANING *he / she sees*

PRONUNCIATION TIP: Like **ви́жу** and **ви́дишь**, the accent is on the first syllable, so it sounds like *V^yEE-d^yeet*.

We're halfway there!

	Singular	Plural
First Person	**я ви́жу**	
Second Person	**ты ви́дишь**	
Third Person	**он/она́ ви́дит**	

Here's an example of a sentence with our new verb for this lesson:

Она́ ви́дит газе́ту. *(She sees the/a newspaper.)*

EXERCISES

1. **Он не ви́дит у́лицу.**
2. **Она́ ви́дит у́лицы.**
3. **Он не ви́дит газе́ту.**
4. **Она́ ви́дит газе́ты.**
5. **Он ви́дит у́лицы и маши́ны.**

6. Он ви́дит маши́ну.

7. Ты ви́дишь у́лицы.

8. Ты ви́дишь газе́ту.

9. Я ви́жу газе́ты.

10. Э́то не Луна́.

Answers on page 256.

LESSON 81

NEW WORD   **мы ви́дим**

MEANING   *we see*

PRONUNCIATION TIP: The accent is on the first syllable, so **ви́дим** sounds something like *VʸEE-dʸeem*.

The chart is getting fuller.

	Singular	Plural
First Person	я ви́жу	мы ви́дим
Second Person	ты ви́дишь	
Third Person	он/она́ ви́дит	

Here's an example of a sentence with our new verb for this lesson:

Мы ви́дим Луну́. *(We see the moon.)*

EXERCISES

1. **Мы ви́дим маши́ну.**
2. **Мы не ви́дим у́лицу.**
3. **Мы ви́дим у́лицы и маши́ны.**
4. **Мы ви́дим газе́ту.**
5. **Мы ви́дим газе́ты.**
6. **Он ви́дит у́лицу.**
7. **Она́ не ви́дит газе́ты.**
8. **Ты ви́дишь Луну́.**
9. **Я ви́жу у́лицу и маши́ны.**
10. **Э́то газе́та.**

Answers on page 257.

LESSON 82

NEW WORD **вы ви́дите**

MEANING *y'all see*

PRONUNCIATION TIP: The word **ви́дите** has three syllables, and sounds something like *V ʸEE-d ʸee-t ʸe*.

	Singular	Plural
First Person	я ви́жу	мы ви́дим
Second Person	ты ви́дишь	вы ви́дите
Third Person	он/она́ ви́дит	

Here's an example of a sentence with our new verb for this lesson:

Вы не ви́дите маши́ну. *(Y'all do not see the/a car.)*

EXERCISES

1. **Вы ви́дите у́лицу и маши́ны.**
2. **Вы не ви́дите маши́ну.**
3. **Вы ви́дите газе́ты.**
4. **Мы ви́дим у́лицу.**
5. **Мы не ви́дим газе́ту.**
6. **Она́ ви́дит газе́ту.**

7. Он ви́дит у́лицы и маши́ны.

8. Ты ви́дишь у́лицу.

9. Я не ви́жу Луну́.

10. Э́то у́лица.

Answers on page 257.

LESSON 83

NEW WORD **они́ ви́дят**

MEANING *they see*

PRONUNCIATION TIP: The accent is on the first syllable, so it sounds like *VʸEE-dʸat*.

	Singular	Plural
First Person	я ви́жу	мы ви́дим
Second Person	ты ви́дишь	вы ви́дите
Third Person	он/она́ ви́дит	они́ ви́дят

Here's an example of a sentence with our new verb for this lesson:

Они́ ви́дят газе́ту. (*They see the/a newspaper.*)

EXERCISES

1. Они́ ви́дят маши́ну.
2. Они́ не ви́дят газе́ты.
3. Вы ви́дите газе́ту.
4. Вы ви́дите у́лицу.
5. Мы ви́дим у́лицы и маши́ны.
6. Она́ ви́дит у́лицы.
7. Он не ви́дит маши́ну.
8. Ты ви́дишь Луну́.
9. Я ви́жу у́лицу и маши́ны.
10. Э́то у́лицы.

Answers on page 257.

LESSON 84

REVIEW

We now know all six present tense forms of **я вѝжу**. Let's review them using the chart below.

	Singular	Plural
First Person	я вѝжу	мы вѝдим
Second Person	ты вѝдишь	вы вѝдите
Third Person	он/онá вѝдит	онѝ вѝдят

Chant and repeat the contents of this chart until you have all the verb forms memorized. Start with the first person singular and go down the first column. Then, go to the top of the plural column. When you chant the pronouns and verbs, it might sounds something like this: **я вѝжу, ты вѝдишь, он/онá вѝдит, мы вѝдим, вы вѝдите, онѝ вѝдят.**

And, as long as we are reviewing things, it's a good idea to keep on reviewing the pronouns you know. Here they are again:

	Singular	Plural
First Person	я	мы
Second Person	ты	вы
Third Person	он/онá	онѝ

Chant them in order, like this: **я, ты, он/она́, мы, вы, они́.**

Another good way to memorize pronouns and verbs (and to improve your reading skills) is to write out the words by hand. At first, it might feel strange writing out unfamiliar words and characters, but as you practice daily, you will improve rapidly. When you write out the words, you use multiple senses at one time: sight, touch, and, when you pronounce what you have written, hearing, too.

LESSON 85

MORE ABOUT DECLENSIONS

For many lessons now, we have been telling you that the endings of Russian nouns change depending on what function a noun performs or what role it plays in a sentence. These different forms are called *cases*. When we use a word as the subject of a sentence, that word is said to be in the nominative case because it just names the person or thing (the word *nominative* is related to the Latin word **nomen** which means "name"). We also use the nominative case for predicate nominatives. When we use a word as a direct object, that word is said to be in the accusative case. In Russian, there are six cases to learn about. Examine the chart below:

	Singular	Plural
Nominative (subject/pred. nom.)	маши́на	маши́ны
Accusative (direct object)	маши́ну	маши́ны

In the chart above, you can see that the names of the various cases are listed in the left-hand column, while singular and plural are indicated at the top. Therefore, this chart makes it easy to view the various forms of each noun. The word **маши́на** is the nominative singular form, **маши́ны** is the nominative plural form, **маши́ну** is the accusative singular form, and **маши́ны** is the accusative plural form. This means that you have experience working with two out of the six cases.

Each case performs certain functions while working together with the other cases to create meaningful sentences. As you learn the remaining cases, you will be able to translate more complex (and interesting) exercises.

LESSON 86

RUSSIAN NAMES

In Russian, personal names are nouns, and they change their case endings just like any other noun. For example, if a person's name is a direct object, the ending of the person's name will change to show that it is in the accusative case.

Since we are working with feminine nouns of the first declension, let's learn some female names that take the endings of the first declension. The name *Anna* is an example of a woman's name from the first declension. In Russian history, the name *Anna* is famous. Anna of Russia (also known as Anna Ivanovna) ruled Russia as empress from 1730 to 1740.

In the chart below, observe the nominative and accusative forms of this name.

Nominative (subject/pred. nom.)	Áнна
Accusative (direct object)	Áнну

Let's look at some examples of how this name could be used in a sentence. Here's an example sentence in which this name is in the nominative case:

Áнна ви́дит маши́ну. *(Anna sees the car.)*

Anna is the subject of the sentence, so her name is in the nominative case. Also notice the third person singular verb. Here's another example, this time with her name in the accusative case:

Мы ви́дим Áнну. *(We see Anna.)*

In that sentence, Anna is the direct object, so the ending of her name changed to **-у** and becomes **Áнну** (pronounced *AHN-ooo*). And here's one last example:

Э́то Áнна. *(This is Anna.* OR *That is Anna.)*

You might say a sentence like this if you are pointing someone out to someone, or introducing someone else. In this context, Anna is the predicate nominative, so the name stays in the nominative form.

Она́ — Áнна. *(She is Anna.)*

Here the pronoun **она́** means *she*, so you are saying *She is Anna*.

EXERCISES

1. **Ты ви́дишь Áнну.**
2. **Áнна ви́дит маши́ну.**
3. **Я ви́жу Áнну.**
4. **Áнна ви́дит газе́ту.**
5. **Вы ви́дите Áнну.**
6. **Э́то Áнна.**
7. **Они́ не ви́дят Áнну.**
8. **Áнна ви́дит у́лицу и маши́ны.**
9. **Он ви́дит Áнну.**
10. **Я — Áнна.**

Answers on page 257.

LESSON 87

INFORMAL RUSSIAN GREETINGS AND PHRASES

In Russian, you can speak either in a casual kind of way, as you would with family and friends, or you can choose to speak in a more formal way, as you might speak to a boss, teacher, or someone you don't know very well. These two kinds of speech are traditionally called informal speech and formal speech.

In this book, so far we have only been working with informal speech. Toward the end of this book, we will teach you a bit about formal speech in Russian and the situations in which you should use it—but for the moment we will be sticking with informal speech. And since you are working with informal speech, we thought you might enjoy learning a few informal Russian greetings and phrases.

First, let's learn how to say *hello* in Russian. Here's an informal greeting you can use with family and friends.

приве́т

It sounds something like *pree-VʸET*. It means roughly the same thing as *Hi!* or *Hello!* in English.

Here's another informal way to say *hello*:

здра́вствуй

This consonant-filled word is quite a mouthful! Despite its length, this word only has two syllables. It starts out with a *z* sound, a *d* sound, and an *r* sound all smooshed together.

Way back in lesson 33, we told you about the letter **й** *(ee kratkoyeh)*. This is the letter that doesn't operate by itself but adds a brief *ee* sound following another vowel. When **й** follows the **у** *(ooh)*, they combine to form the sound *oo-ey*. It is pronounced quickly and could end up sounding more like *oy*. Therefore, the word sounds something like *ZDRAH-stvooy*. You can use it just as you would use the word *hello* in English.

To say a quick goodbye to friends or family, say this:

пока́

The **o** in the first syllable of this word is in an unstressed syllable—therefore this word sounds something like *pah-KAH*. In the answer key, we will translate it as *Bye!*

Here is how to say *thank you* in Russian (you may remember that we mentioned this in lesson 32):

спаси́бо

This word sounds something like *spah-SEE-buh*, with the accent on the second syllable. This expression is a shortened version of the longer expression **спаси вас Бог** which means *May God save you*. But over time it was shortened to **спаси́бо**.

Finally, you will want to know how to say *You're welcome* in response:

пожа́луйста

This word sounds something like *pah-ZHAHL-stuh*. It is used in various situations but is always an appropriate response to **спаси́бо**.

EXERCISES

1. Приве́т!
2. Пока́.
3. Спаси́бо.
4. Пока́, А́нна.
5. Я ви́жу А́нну.
6. Здра́вствуй!
7. Мы ви́дим маши́ны и у́лицы.
8. Ты ви́дишь А́нну.
9. Они́ ви́дят газе́ты.
10. Э́то А́нна.

Answers on page 257.

LESSON 88

MORE RUSSIAN NAMES

In this lesson, let's learn two more Russian female names: *Clara* and *Olga*.

Clara looks like this: **Кла́ра**. Notice that this word does not sound like the English name Clara. For starters, the first vowel in **Кла́ра** sounds like the *a* in *father*. Second, the *r* sound in this word is not pronounced the way an English speaker would pronounce it, like the *urrr* sound at the beginning of the word *rainbow*. Instead, the *r* sound in this word is only a light tap of the tongue against the roof of the mouth, almost like a quick *d* sound. Therefore the word **Кла́ра** sounds something like *KLAH-da*.

Olga looks like this: **О́льга**. This name has the soft sign in it, right after the letter **л** *(el)*. This means that the letter **л** *(el)* will be soft (palatalized), and so you should pronounce it with your tongue raised to the roof of your mouth. Notice that this is rather different from the way the name *Olga* would be pronounced in English.

As you know, Russian names take the same endings as any other Russian nouns. In these charts you can see the nominative and accusative forms of these names.

Nominative (subject/pred. nom.)	Кла́ра
Accusative (direct object)	Кла́ру

Nominative (subject/pred. nom.)	О́льга
Accusative (direct object)	О́льгу

EXERCISES

1. Óльга ви́дит А́нну.
2. А́нна ви́дит О́льгу.
3. О́льга не ви́дит Луну́.
4. Кла́ра ви́дит О́льгу и А́нну.
5. Они́ ви́дят Кла́ру.
6. Кла́ра ви́дит газе́ту.
7. Приве́т, О́льга!
8. Э́то Кла́ра.
9. Спаси́бо, О́льга.
10. Пока́.

Answers on page 257.

LESSON 89

MY NAME IS...

In English, if you want to tell someone what your name is, you'll construct a sentence like this:

My name is Anna.

But in Russian this kind of sentence would be worded differently. Here is a word-for-word translation of how you would structure this sentence in Russian:

Me they call Anna.

The Russian word for *me* is **меня** which sounds like *mee-N^YA*. (Just for fun, we would also like to mention that **меня** is accusative.)

Next, the word **зовут** is a verb that means *they call*. This word sounds something like *zah-VOOT*.

If you put these words together with the name Anna, here is what you get:

Меня́ зову́т А́нна.

Try using this phrase with your own name!

EXERCISES

1. **Меня́ зову́т А́нна.**
2. **Меня́ зову́т О́льга.**
3. **Меня́ зову́т Кла́ра.**
4. **Спаси́бо, О́льга.**
5. **Пока́, О́льга.**
6. **Пока́, А́нна.**

7. Э́то у́лица.

8. Мы ви́дим у́лицы и маши́ны.

9. А́нна не ви́дит маши́ну.

10. Они́ ви́дят газе́ты.

Answers on page 258.

LESSON 90

NEW WORD **я чита́ю**

MEANING *I read, I am reading*

PRONUNCIATION TIP: The word **чита́ю** sounds like *chi-TAH-yoo*.

In the past we gave you the forms of **я ви́жу** one form at a time. But now that you have had some experience working with verbs and pronouns, it's no longer necessary to give you one form at a time. So here are all six present tense forms of our new verb for this lesson.

	Singular	Plural
First Person	я чита́ю	мы чита́ем
Second Person	ты чита́ешь	вы чита́ете
Third Person	он/она́ чита́ет	они́ чита́ют

Here's an example of how you might use this verb in a sentence:

Я чита́ю газе́ту. *(I am reading the/a newspaper.)*

Notice that in our example sentence, the word for *newspaper* was in the accusative case because it is a direct object.

EXERCISES

1. **Я чита́ю газе́ту.**
2. **Кла́ра чита́ет газе́ты.**
3. **Мы чита́ем газе́ту.**
4. **Ты не чита́ешь газе́ты.**
5. **О́льга чита́ет газе́ту.**
6. **Меня́ зову́т О́льга.**
7. **Пока́, Кла́ра.**
8. **Спаси́бо, А́нна.**
9. **О́льга ви́дит Кла́ру. О́льга не ви́дит А́нну.**
10. **Пока́, А́нна.**

Answers on page 258.

LESSON 91

THE PRESENT TENSE

In this book, all the verbs that we will learn about are present tense verbs. This means that the action happening is in the here and now. But did you know that there is more than one kind of present tense?

In English, you might see a sentence like this:

> I read the newspaper.

The person saying that sentence may not be reading a newspaper right this minute, but it is still an activity that this person does at times. This kind of present tense is called the *simple present*. Contrast that with this similar English sentence:

> I am reading the newspaper.

In this sentence, someone is saying that the activity of reading the newspaper is ongoing right now! This kind of present tense is called the *present progressive*. It's progressive because the action is ongoing at this very moment.

How does this relate to Russian verbs? What we want you to understand is that in English, there is both a simple present and a present progressive, but in Russian there is not. In Russian, there is only one way to say something in the present tense. Observe this Russian sentence:

> **Я чита́ю газе́ту.**

If you translate this sentence into English, you could translate it as either *I read the newspaper* or *I am reading the newspaper*. How will you know whether to translate a verb using simple present or present progressive? Look at the context, and that should make it clear. For example, if you saw a Russian sentence that says **Я чита́ю** and you aren't sure what the best translation is, try translating it as both *I read* and *I am reading* and see which one sounds better. But if there is no context, you just have to make a judgment call and go with it.

LESSON 92

VERB STEMS AND PERSONAL ENDINGS

You may have noticed by now that there is a pattern to the endings of Russian verbs. For instance, first person plural verbs always end in **-м**, as seen in words like **ви́дим** and **чита́ем**. Also, second person singular verbs always end in **-шь** as seen in words like **ви́дишь** and **чита́ешь**. Why is this?

The reason for this is that Russian verbs are constructed with two main parts: a stem and an ending. You have already seen this concept with Russian nouns. A Russian noun has a stem, and then we add the appropriate ending to the stem depending on whether the noun is nominative, accusative, etc. Russian verbs work the same way. Each verb has a stem, and we add endings to that stem.

In order to learn more about Russian verb stems and endings, let's take a closer look at the verb **чита́ю** for a moment. Study each form of this verb and see if you can figure out what the stem of the verb is.

	Singular	Plural
First Person	я чита́ю	мы чита́ем
Second Person	ты чита́ешь	вы чита́ете
Third Person	он/она́ чита́ет	они́ чита́ют

Notice that each form of **чита́ю** starts with **чита-**. That is the stem of the verb. But what about the end of the verb? What's that all about?

After the stem, each different form of the verb has its own special, individual ending. We call these endings *personal endings*. If we isolated those endings and put them into a chart, it would look like this:

	Singular	Plural
First Person	**-ю**	**-ем**
Second Person	**-ешь**	**-ете**
Third Person	**-ет**	**-ют**

These personal endings vary a little from verb to verb, but mostly they stay the same, so it's a good idea to study them and memorize them.

A few lessons ago, we mentioned that in Russian you are not required to use pronouns with verbs. In other words, **читáю** means *I read* on its own, even without the pronoun **я**. Likewise, the second person singular form **читáешь** means *you read* even without the pronoun **ты**, and so on and so forth. Now in this lesson, hopefully you are starting to get a fuller picture of why this is true—because the endings of verbs indicate who is doing the action. Pronouns can be very helpful! They can help a speaker or writer to be specific and avoid ambiguity. But even without the help of a pronoun, Russian verbs show who is doing the action because of their special endings.

Now that you know about verb stems and personal endings, let's work with them a little and try to build some different forms of **читáю**. Say, for example, that you wanted to create the second person singular form of **читáю**. First you would take the stem of the verb:

чита-

Then you would find the personal ending for the second person singular:

-ешь

Now put them together, like this:

чита + **ешь** = **читáешь**

Just for practice, take some time to experiment with this concept. Get out a pen and some paper and start writing! Write out the stem of the verb, thinking of what form you want to make, and then add the personal ending for that particular form. After a while, see if you can do it from memory—use the chart to check yourself afterward.

LESSON 93

MORE ABOUT VERB STEMS AND PERSONAL ENDINGS

In the last lesson, you learned about verb stems and personal endings. We mentioned that the stem stays the same for every form of the verb, and that the personal endings stay mostly the same from verb to verb, but that they do change a little.

So now that you know those basic concepts, we would like to do the same kind of examination of the other verb you know, which is **я вижу**. This verb is a bit more complicated than **я читаю** because it has a slightly different structure. Let's start out our close examination of **я вижу** by examining its various present tense forms. Examine each form closely. Can you figure out which part of the verb is the stem and which part is the personal ending? Why or why not?

	Singular	Plural
First Person	я вижу	мы видим
Second Person	ты видишь	вы видите
Third Person	он/она видит	они видят

OK, that was kind of a trick question. You may have had some trouble figuring out what the stem of the verb is because it's not the same for every form. That's because this particular verb is what we call a *stem-changing verb*. For the first person singular form, the stem is this:

виж-

But for the other five present tense forms of the verb, the stem is this:

вид-

So, because **ви́жу** is a stem-changing verb, you will need to be aware of what the two stems are, and when to use them.

Another thing to know about this verb is that the personal endings are slightly different than for **чита́ю**. For the sake of comparison, let's put the personal endings for **ви́жу** and **чита́ю** side by side.

ви́жу	Singular	Plural
1	**-у**	**-им**
2	**-ишь**	**-ите**
3	**-ит**	**-ят**

чита́ю	Singular	Plural
1	**-ю**	**-ем**
2	**-ешь**	**-ете**
3	**-ет**	**-ют**

First, a general observation. Notice that the consonants in the personal endings are the same, but the vowels are the letters that tend to change. For example, take a look at the third person singular endings. They each end with the same consonant, which is the letter **т** *(te)*. But the vowel before the **т** *(te)* is different. For **ви́жу** the vowel is **и** *(ee)* but for **чита́ю** the vowel is **е** *(yeh)*. So even though the final consonant in that ending is the same for both, the vowel that comes before it is different. And this is the same with the second person singular, first person plural, second person plural, and third person plural. In the first person singular, there is no consonant, so the entire ending is different.

It is beyond the scope of this short book to go into too much detail about Russian verb forms, but we do at least want to make you aware of some of the most general concepts so that you can keep them in mind as you continue with your Russian studies.

LESSON 94

EVEN MORE RUSSIAN NAMES

The Russian way to say *Catherine* is **Екатери́на** (pronounced *yeh-ka-tʸe-REE-na*). This was the name of the famous Catherine the Great, who ruled as Empress of Russia from 1762 until 1796. After deposing her husband in a *coup d'état*, Catherine presided over Russian territorial expansion during her long reign. A common nickname version of **Екатери́на** is **Ка́тя** (pronounced *KAH-tʸa*).

Another common Russian female name is **Ната́ша** (pronounced *na-TAH-shah*). This name is a nickname version of the name Natalia, which is **Ната́лья** in Russian.

Another common Russian name is **Светла́на** (pronounced *svet-LAH-na*). It is based upon the root word *svet* which means *light,* so the name Svetlana conveys the idea of light or purity. The nickname version of **Светла́на** is **Све́та** (pronounced *SVʸE-tah*).

EXERCISES

1. **Екатери́на чита́ет газе́ту.**
2. **Меня́ зову́т Светла́на.**
3. **Они́ не ви́дят Ната́шу.**
4. **Э́то Екатери́на.**
5. **Светла́на ви́дит Ната́шу и Екатери́ну.**
6. **Мы ви́дим Светла́ну.**
7. **Пока́, Ната́ша.**
8. **Э́то О́льга.**
9. **Пока́, Светла́на.**
10. **Приве́т, О́льга!**

Answers on page 258.

LESSON 95

SPELLING RULES

It's time for you to take your knowledge of Russian to the next level! But in order to do that, we need to teach you about some spelling variations that commonly occur in Russian. These variations are governed by certain rules called *spelling rules*. Because of these spelling rules, there will be some variation in the endings for the declension we are teaching you—in other words, the first declension ending pattern will not be exactly the same for every noun.

In English, we have a few general spelling rules (with many exceptions), but not really the same kinds of spelling rules found in Russian. However, there are some spelling patterns in English that look to us like unwritten spelling rules. Just for fun (and to mentally prepare you for Russian spelling rules), let's look at one particular example of how English words conform to certain spelling patterns.

Think for a moment about words that start with the prefix *con-*, like these words:

- connection
- contempt
- confession
- concept
- contingent

All these words come to us from Latin, so the pattern we are examining here should perhaps be viewed as more of a Latin spelling convention rather than an English one. Anyway, these words consist of the prefix *con-* and then a root word. For example, in the word *connection* we have the prefix *con-* plus a form of the root word *nexus*.

But if the prefix *con-* is attached to the beginning of a root word that starts with the letter *p*, something special happens. Observe these words and see if you can figure out what is going on with the spelling:

- compression
- companion
- computer
- complex
- composite
- component

You probably noticed that when the root word starts with the letter *p* the spelling of the *con-* prefix changes from *con-* to *com-*. So why does the *n* turn into an *m*?

The reason that the *n* changes to an *m* is so that the word is easier to pronounce. When you say a *p* sound, your lips must come together so you can send out a puff of air, making a "puh" sound. But when you say an *n* sound, your lips are in a completely different position. Just for fun, try to say a few of these words with the prefix *con-* instead of *com-*. What do you notice?

- conpression / compression
- conpanion / companion
- conputer / computer
- conplex / complex
- conposite / composite
- conponent / component

What you may have noticed is that when the prefix *con-* is followed by the letter *p*, it is more difficult to say because your lips have to make a big move going from the *n* sound to the *p* sound. But on the other hand, when the *n* changes to an *m*, the word becomes easier to say because when you say the *mmm* sound of the letter *m*, your lips are already together, ready to make the *p* sound. In other words, your lips are already in place for the *p* and they don't have to make a big change.

Therefore, if we were to try to make a spelling rule out of this phenomenon, we could say this:

Before the letter *p*, the letter *n* changes to an *m*.

Here is the point we are trying to communicate: in the Russian language, there are spelling rules that dictate what sounds and letters can come after other sounds and letters. And, as we mentioned before, because of these rules there will be some variation to the declension endings of nouns. In the next lesson, you will learn the first Russian spelling rule.

LESSON 96

SPELLING RULE #1

In the last lesson, we used some example words from English to introduce you to the concept of spelling rules. You learned that in English, the letter *n* in the prefix *con-* changes to an *m* when the root word it's attached to begins with the letter *p*. It's not exactly a spelling rule, but it's close enough to use as an example so you can grasp the concept.

Now it's time to introduce you to your first Russian spelling rule. Some sources call it Spelling Rule #1, while others call it the Seven-Letter Rule. Here it is:

> Spelling rule #1: after the letters **Г** *(ghe)*, **К** *(kah)*, **Х** *(cha)*, **Ж** *(zhe)*, **Ч** *(cheh)*, **Ш** *(shah)*, and **Щ** *(shsha)*, you cannot put the vowel **Ы** *(y)*. In its place you must put the letter **И** *(ee)*.

In order to help you learn this new spelling rule, we would like to teach you a new noun: the word **книга** which means *book*. The **К** *(kah)* at the beginning of this word is not silent, so this word sounds something like *k-NEE-ga* with the *k* sound and the *n* sound pronounced together, in quick succession. The nominative plural form **книги**, with the the letter **И** *(ee)* at the end, sounds something like *k-NEE-gee*.

The stem of this noun is **книг-**. Notice that the last letter of the stem is the letter **Г** *(ghe)*. This is one of the letters mentioned in spelling rule #1.

Let's do a little experiment. Let's say that you want to make the nominative plural form of **книга,** so you take the stem...

   книг-

...and then you take the nominative plural ending for the first declension...

   -ы

And you put it all together to make the nominative plural form. What will happen?

   книг + ы = ~~книгы~~

Noooooo! You can't add the ending **ы** *(y)* to the stem **книг-** because it violates the spelling rule. Instead of **ы** *(y)* as the nominative plural ending, you must put the letter **и** *(ee)* as the ending for the nominative plural form of **кни́га,** like this:

книг + и = кни́ги ☺

Let's take what we have so far and put it into a declension chart. Notice that the letter **и** *(ee)* is the ending in both the nominative plural and accusative plural forms (those forms are circled in the chart).

	Singular	Plural
Nominative (subject/pred. nom.)	кни́га	кни́ги
Accusative (direct object)	кни́гу	кни́ги

See if you can identify these forms of **кни́га** as you translate the exercises.

EXERCISES

1. **кни́га**
2. **кни́ги**
3. **Я чита́ю кни́гу.**
4. **Ты чита́ешь кни́ги.**
5. **Она́ чита́ет кни́ги и газе́ты.**
6. **Мы не чита́ем газе́ту.**

7. Меня́ зову́т Екатери́на.

8. Спаси́бо, Кла́ра. Пока́.

9. Здра́вствуй. Меня́ зову́т Екатери́на. Э́то О́льга.

10. Ната́ша не ви́дит Луну́. Вы ви́дете Луну́ и у́лицы.

Answers on page 258.

LESSON 97

NEW WORD **покупа́ю**

MEANING *I buy*

PRONUNCIATION TIP: This verb has four syllables, and the accent is on the third syllable. Therefore **покупа́ю** sounds something like *puh-koo-PAH-yoo*.

	Singular	Plural
First Person	я покупа́ю	мы покупа́ем
Second Person	ты покупа́ешь	вы покупа́ете
Third Person	он/она́ покупа́ет	они́ покупа́ют

Here's an example of how you might use this verb in a sentence:

Я покупа́ю кни́гу. *(I am buying the/a book.)*

EXERCISES

1. Светла́на покупа́ет кни́гу.
2. Мы не покупа́ем маши́ну.
3. Екатери́на не покупа́ет газе́ту. Она́ покупа́ет кни́гу.
4. Вы чита́ете кни́ги и газе́ты.
5. Приве́т. Меня́ зову́т Светла́на.
6. Они́ чита́ют кни́ги.
7. Э́то газе́ты. Мы чита́ем газе́ты.
8. Светла́на ви́дит Екатери́ну и Ната́шу.
9. Я — Екатери́на. Я — не Ната́ша.
10. Ты ви́дишь О́льгу.

Answers on page 258.

LESSON 98

NEW WORD **бума́га**

MEANING *paper*

PRONUNCIATION TIP: This word sounds something like *boo-MAH-ga*.

Our new word for this lesson is a noun that means *paper* (meaning the substance known as paper, not an individual piece of paper such as a document or newspaper). Examine the stem of **бума́га** and see if you can figure out how it is similar to the word **кни́га** *(book)* which you learned a couple of lessons ago:

бума́г-

As we saw with **кни́га**, the stem of **бума́га** ends with the letter **г** *(ghe)*. This means that because of spelling rule #1, it cannot have the letter **ы** *(y)* as its nominative plural or accusative plural ending. Instead, like **кни́га**, it will have **и** *(ee)*. You can see this reflected in the declension chart below.

	Singular	Plural
Nominative (subject/pred. nom.)	бума́га	бума́ги
Accusative (direct object)	бума́гу	бума́ги

Here's an example of how **бума́га** could be used in a sentence:

Я покупа́ю бума́гу. *(I am buying (the) paper.)*

EXERCISES

1. **Ты покупа́ешь бума́гу.**
2. **Светла́на ви́дит кни́ги и бума́гу.**
3. **Они́ не ви́дят бума́гу.**
4. **Э́то газе́ты. Мы чита́ем газе́ты.**
5. **Ната́ша чита́ет кни́гу.**
6. **Приве́т, Екатери́на.**
7. **Меня́ зову́т О́льга. Э́то Кла́ра.**
8. **Вы не чита́ете кни́ги.**
9. **Они́ покупа́ют газе́ты и кни́ги.**
10. **Спаси́бо, Ната́ша.**

Answers on page 259.

LESSON 99

ANIMATE NOUNS VS. INANIMATE NOUNS

The word *animate* comes to us from the Latin word **anima** which can mean things like *soul, spirit,* or *life.* Therefore an animate object is something that is a living, moving thing, but an inanimate object is not alive. We have many English words related to the Latin word **anima**, such as *animation, animal, unanimous,* and one of our personal favorites, *magnanimous.*

A few lessons ago we told you that there would be some variation to the endings of the first declension. In other words, the pattern of endings that you learn for one particular noun may not be the same for every noun. In fact, you have already seen this happen with the nouns **книга** and **бумага** because of spelling rule #1. But spelling rules are not the only factors that will cause there to be variations in the pattern of endings for the first declension. Another factor will be whether or not a noun is animate.

Many of the first declension nouns we have taught you so far are inanimate objects: things like books, paper, cars, streets, etc. You know a few names too, but so far you haven't learned any first declension nouns that designate people—in other words, terms such as *woman, girl, grandmother,* or *sister* (we are setting aside the masculine nouns we taught you earlier).

But that is going to change soon. In the next lesson, you will learn the Russian word for *woman,* and as you do you will have to learn about the differences in endings between animate and inanimate nouns in Russian.

LESSON 100

NEW WORD **же́нщина**

MEANING *woman*

PRONUNCIATION TIP: Our new word for this lesson contains a letter that you haven't had a chance to use yet. It's the letter *shsha*, which looks like this: **щ**. This letter makes a *sh* sound in the very front of the mouth, as in the expression *fresh sheets*. The word **же́нщина** has the stress on the first syllable, so it sounds something like *ZHEN-shee-na*. The letter **ж** *(zhe)* is always hard, so the fact that it is followed by the letter **е** *(yeh)* will not cause it to be palatalized.

In the last lesson, we told you that the declension pattern for animate nouns is different from that of inanimate nouns. Therefore, in this lesson you will be learning an animate noun so you can practice this declension pattern. Here is a declension chart for **же́нщина**, which is our new word for this lesson. The stem of this noun is **же́нщин-**. Take a moment to look at the various endings (especially the circled one) and see if you notice anything.

	Singular	Plural
Nominative (subject/pred. nom.)	же́нщина	же́нщины
Accusative (direct object)	же́нщину	(же́нщин)

Did you notice anything strange about that noun's endings? The thing that we wanted you to notice is that **же́нщина** has the usual endings for the nominative singular, nominative plural, and accusative singular. But in the accusative plural, it has no ending at all. We told you that the stem of the noun is **же́нщин-** and so you would expect to see some kind of ending added to that stem in each form of the noun—but in the accusative plural, there is nothing after the stem. In Russian grammar, when a noun has no ending after the stem, it is called a *zero ending*.

Let's see this accusative plural form with the zero ending in a real sentence. Here's a sentence to practice with:

Мы ви́дим же́нщин. *(We see (the) women.)*

From now on, whenever you learn a new noun that is animate, watch out for the zero ending in the accusative plural form. In the exercises below, can you correctly identify and translate the various forms of **же́нщина**?

EXERCISES

1. А́нна — же́нщина.
2. Мы — же́нщины.
3. Мы ви́дим же́нщину.
4. Мы ви́дим же́нщин.
5. Они́ не же́нщины.
6. Же́нщины покупа́ют кни́ги.
7. Же́нщина покупа́ет газе́ту.
8. Ты же́нщина.
9. Екатери́на и О́льга — же́нщины.
10. Спаси́бо, О́льга. Пока́.

Answers on page 259.

LESSON 101

NEW WORD **актри́са**

MEANING *actress*

PRONUNCIATION TIP: The accent is on the second syllable, so this word sounds something like *ahk-TREE-sa*.

In the last lesson, you learned that animate nouns of the first declension will have something called a zero ending in the accusative plural form. This means that the accusative plural form is the same as the stem of the noun. The stem of **актри́са** is **актри́с-**, so that is what you should expect to see as the accusative plural form of this noun.

	Singular	Plural
Nominative (subject/pred. nom.)	актри́са	актри́сы
Accusative (direct object)	актри́су	(актри́с)

EXERCISES

1. **Екатери́на актри́са.**
2. **Же́нщины — актри́сы.**
3. **Они́ ви́дят актри́су.**

4. Мы не ви́дим актри́с.

5. Ты актри́са.

6. Здра́вствуй. Меня́ зову́т О́льга. Я актри́са.

7. Же́нщина актри́са.

8. Ната́ша и Светла́на актри́сы.

9. Мы покупа́ем бума́гу.

10. Я чита́ю кни́гу. Пока́!

Answers on page 259.

LESSON 102

THE CONJUNCTION "BUT"

In English the word *but* can be used in different ways. For example, *but* can mean *however*, as when something is contrary to what is expected:

This store has very low prices, <u>but</u> Sheila isn't buying anything.

Since the prices at the store are so low, you might expect that Sheila would buy something under those circumstances. Therefore, the fact that Sheila isn't buying anything is contrary to our expectations. So we could reword that sentence using the word *however* in place of *but*, like this:

This store has very low prices; <u>however</u>, Sheila isn't buying anything.

The word *but* can also be used to mean something like *while* or *on the other hand*. This is done when the contrast is not as strong, and there aren't really any expectations for what should be happening.

Bob has a blender, <u>but</u> he doesn't have a toaster oven.

In that sentence, there is no expectation that Bob would have any particular kitchen appliances—the two parts of the sentence are simply conveying information about what appliances he does or does not have. Therefore, we could reword that sentence, replacing the word *but* with the word *while* or with the phrase *on the other hand*, like this:

Bob has a blender, <u>while</u> he doesn't have a toaster oven.

In Russian, there are two different words that can be translated into English as *but*. The first one is the word **но**. It sounds like the English word *no*, but with the jaw more open, and with your lips moving outward. This word corresponds to the first meaning of the word *but* that we demonstrated above—the one that means *however*. Here's how we can use **но** in a Russian sentence:

Я читáю газéты, но я не читáю кнúги. *(I read (the) newspapers, but I do not read (the) books.)*

In the first part of that sentence, we find out that the speaker reads newspapers. For this reason, you might expect that this person is an avid reader, reading all kinds of things. But in the second part of the sentence, we find out that the speaker does not read books. That might go against the expectation set up by the first part of the sentence. Therefore, the appropriate word for *but* there was the word **но**. Also notice that since the statements in this example are general statements, we translated **я читáю** as *I read* instead of *I am reading*.

The other way to say *but* in Russian is with the word **а** (which is also a letter of the alphabet). It sounds like the *a* in *father*. This word corresponds to the second meaning of the word *but* that we demonstrated above—the one that means *while* or *on the other hand*. We can use it in a sentence when the second part of the sentence states information that is different somehow from the first part of the sentence, but doesn't really conflict with it in any way. Here's an example:

Я читáю газéты, а ты не читáешь газéты. *(I read (the) newspapers, but you do not read (the) newspapers.)*

In that example, in the first part of the sentence we find out that the speaker reads newspapers. So far so good. Then, the speaker says that the person listening (you) does not read newspapers. Therefore, there is a contrast between the first and second parts of the sentence, but the two parts of the sentence are not necessarily related to each other or in conflict with each other. In fact, the sentence would mean basically the same thing if you used the word *and* instead of *but*, like this: *I read newspapers and you do not read newspapers.* For this reason, the word **а** can sometimes be translated into English as *and*.

The example sentences we gave you above aren't exactly ideal because at this point in your Russian studies you still have a very limited vocabulary. So it's hard to create a strong context in which to use **но** and **а**. But we at least wanted to introduce you to these two words so you can begin practicing with them and getting accustomed to their different shades of meaning. The good news is that in this book, both of these words will translate into English as *but*, and that's how these words will be represented in the answer key (we won't use **а** as *and*). The exercises will strive to use each of these words in their appropriate situations, so be on the lookout for them. No "buts" about it!

EXERCISES

1. Я актри́са, а ты не актри́са.
2. Екатери́на актри́са, а Ната́ша не актри́са.
3. Мы ви́дим Светла́ну, но мы не ви́дим Кла́ру.
4. Ната́ша чита́ет кни́ги, но она́ не чита́ет газе́ты.
5. Вы покупа́ете маши́ну, а мы покупа́ем кни́ги.
6. А́нна не актри́са.
7. Э́то — Ната́ша. Она́ — актри́са.
8. Вы не чита́ете газе́ты, но вы покупа́ете газе́ту.
9. Екатери́на и О́льга — же́нщины.
10. Ната́ша не ви́дит же́нщин.

Answers on page 259.

LESSON 103

NEW WORD **собáка**

MEANING *dog*

PRONUNCIATION TIP: The accent is on the second syllable, so it sounds something like *sa-BAH-ka*.

Our new noun for this lesson might give you a "ruff" time because its declension pattern will be affected by two different considerations. First of all, let's review spelling rule #1:

Spelling rule #1: after the letters **Г** *(ghe)*, **К** *(kah)*, **Х** *(cha)*, **Ж** *(zhe)*, **Ч** *(cheh)*, **Ш** *(shah)*, and **Щ** *(shsha)*, you cannot put the vowel **Ы** *(y)*. In its place you must put the letter **И** *(ee)*.

And now, let's take a look at the stem of the noun **собáка**:

собáк-

The last letter of the stem is the letter **К** *(kah)* which is one of the letters mentioned in spelling rule #1. This means that you cannot put the letter **Ы** *(y)* after it. Instead, you must put the letter **И** *(ee)* as the ending for the nominative plural. This is circled in the chart below.

	SINGULAR	PLURAL
NOMINATIVE (SUBJECT/PRED. NOM.)	собáка	собáки
ACCUSATIVE (DIRECT OBJECT)	собáку	собáк

The other factor that will affect the endings of **собáка** is the fact that it is an animate noun. Therefore, the accusative plural form will have the zero ending. This means that the accusative plural form will be spelled the same as the stem of the noun. This is also circled in the chart shown above.

EXERCISES

1. Екатерина покупáет собáк.
2. Вы не вѝдите собáку.
3. Э́то собáка.
4. Собáка вѝдит А́нну.
5. Жéнщины вѝдят собáк.
6. Мы покупáем собáку, но вы не покупáете собáку.
7. Светлáна — актрѝса.
8. Актрѝсы вѝдят жéнщин.
9. Собáки вѝдят бумáгу.
10. Жéнщины читáют кнѝги. Онѝ не читáют газéты.

Answers on page 260.

LESSON 104

THE FEMININE ENDING -ка

In Russian, many nouns that refer to people occur in male/female pairs. The female version of the word sometimes adds a special feminine ending, which is **-ка**.

Below, compare the word for a male university student with the word for a female university student. Notice that they are the same except that the feminine version has the **-ка** ending.

- **студе́нт**
- **студе́нтка**

As you might expect, the word **студе́нтка** is a first declension feminine noun. But there is one variation in the declension pattern that we need to tell you about. Examine this declension chart for **студе́нтка**, paying special attention to the accusative plural form.

	Singular	Plural
Nominative (subject/pred. nom.)	студе́нтка	студе́нтки
Accusative (direct object)	студе́нтку	(студе́нток)

The stem of **студе́нтка** is **студе́нтк-**. Since the last letter of the stem is **к** (kah), this means that spelling rule #1 applies—but you are already familiar with that.

150

What is new about this particular noun is that there is an extra letter inserted into the accusative plural form. You learned earlier that with animate nouns, the accusative plural form looks just like the stem of the noun, with what is called the zero ending. Just for fun, try to pronounce the stem of **студе́нтка**. Here it is again:

студе́нтк-

With the **т** *(te)* and the **к** *(kah)* right next to each other, it is rather difficult to pronounce. For this reason, an **о** *(oh)* gets inserted between them, making pronunciation much smoother. So the accusative plural form is **студе́нток**.

EXERCISES

1. **А́нна студе́нтка.**
2. **Же́нщины — студе́нтки.**
3. **Мы ви́дим студе́нток.**
4. **Соба́ка — не студе́нтка!**
5. **Ната́ша студе́нтка, а Кла́ра не студе́нтка.**
6. **Студе́нтки покупа́ют кни́ги.**
7. **Актри́са ви́дит соба́к.**
8. **Актри́са же́нщина.**
9. **Э́то студе́нтка.**
10. **Я чита́ю кни́гу.**

Answers on page 260.

LESSON 105

NEW WORD **журнали́стка**

MEANING *female journalist*

Like **студе́нтка**, the word for this lesson is formed by adding the special **-ка** ending to a masculine noun. In this case, it is added to the word for journalist, which you learned earlier in the book. Compare these two forms:

- **журнали́ст**
- **журнали́стка**

A difference to point out here is that while **студе́нт** and **студе́нтка** must be used for male and female university students, respectively, the distinction with the **журнали́ст**/**журнали́стка** pair is not as strict. As language changes over time, it is becoming more common to use the masculine form of certain words for either gender. Therefore, the word **журнали́ст** could actually refer to either a male or female journalist. We are using the word **журнали́стка** to help you study the Russian language, but don't be surprised if you see a female journalist referred to as a **журнали́ст**.

Again, as we saw with **студе́нтка**, the accusative plural has the letter **о** *(oh)* inserted between the **т** *(te)* and the **к** *(kah)*.

	Singular	Plural
Nominative (subject/pred. nom.)	журнали́стка	журнали́стки
Accusative (direct object)	журнали́стку	журнали́сток

EXERCISES

1. Ольга журналистка, а Екатерина актриса.
2. Я вижу журналисток.
3. Вы не видите журналистку.
4. Клара не журналистка.
5. Екатерина — женщина и журналистка.
6. Собаки видят женщину.
7. Анна студентка и актриса.
8. Мы не студентки. Пока.
9. Женщина читает книгу.
10. Это Наташа. Она журналистка.

Answers on page 260.

LESSON 106

NEW WORD **спортсме́нка**

MEANING *female athlete*

PRONUNCIATION TIP: The letter **е** *(yeh)* in this word indicates that the **м** *(em)* just before it is soft (palatalized). Therefore this word sounds something like *sports-MʸEN-ka*.

The word **спортсме́н** is the Russian word for *athlete*. As you might guess, it's a loan word from English, specifically the word *sportsman*. Although it might sound kind of funny to English speakers, adding the feminine ending **-ка** to this word makes it feminine, with the meaning *female athlete*.

спортсме́н ⟶ спортсме́нка

The stem of **спортсме́нка** is **спортсме́нк-**. As seen with **студе́нтка** and **журнали́стка**, the letter **о** *(oh)* is added to the accusative plural form between the last two letters of the stem.

	Singular	Plural
Nominative (subject/pred. nom.)	спортсме́нка	спортсме́нки
Accusative (direct object)	спортсме́нку	спортсме́нок

EXERCISES

1. О́льга спортсме́нка.
2. Кла́ра и А́нна — спортсме́нки.
3. Светла́на ви́дит спортсме́нку.
4. Журнали́стка ви́дит спортсме́нок.
5. Вы не ви́дите студе́нток.
6. Соба́ки ви́дят актри́с.
7. Э́то Екатери́на и Ната́ша. Они́ студе́нтки.
8. Мы ви́дим журнали́сток.
9. Вы — же́нщины.
10. Ты спортсме́нка, а я актри́са.

Answers on page 260.

LESSON 107

POSSESSION

Possessive words show ownership of something. In English, we often show possession by using an apostrophe followed by the letter *s*. Observe the following examples:

- Fred's car
- The nation's flag
- Arizona's capital

Sometimes we show possession by using the word *of*.

- The peak of the mountain
- The smell of garlic
- The beginning of the show

Therefore, in English, when you want to show possession of something, you must decide whether to use an apostrophe or the word *of*.

Here are a few of the most basic rules to remember when using apostrophes:

	Rule	Example
Rule #1	To make a noun that does not end in *s* possessive, just add an apostrophe and an *s*.	Lauren always wants to borrow Kate's Russian book.
Rule #2	To make a singular noun that ends in *s* possessive, add an apostrophe and an *s* (just like rule #1).	The class's favorite subject was Russian.
Rule #3	To make a plural noun that ends in *s* possessive, add an apostrophe to the end of the word.	Due to increased interest in Russian, all the books' covers are starting to wear out.

LESSON 108

THE GENITIVE CASE

The case on the second row of our chart is called the genitive case. This case is used to show possession. When you translate the genitive case into English, you will need to use one of the following two methods:

- An apostrophe and the letter *s*
- The word *of*

A genitive noun that is possessing something usually comes right after the word it is possessing. Note that this is the opposite of how we often do it in English. For example, in the phrase *Fred's car* the possessive word comes before thing it possesses.

In the first declension (the only declension we will cover in this book), the genitive singular will *always* look the same as the nominative plural. In the chart below, notice that the nominative plural and genitive singular forms of **маши́на** look identical.

	Singular	Plural
Nominative (subject/pred. nom.)	маши́на	маши́ны
Genitive (possession)	маши́ны	
Accusative (direct object)	маши́ну	маши́ны

For nouns that obey spelling rule #1, the nominative plural and genitive singular will look the same, too. In the chart below, notice that **соба́ки** is both the nominative plural and genitive singular form of **соба́ка**.

	Singular	Plural
Nominative (subject/pred. nom.)	соба́ка	⟨соба́ки⟩
Genitive (possession)	⟨соба́ки⟩	
Accusative (direct object)	соба́ку	соба́к

You may be wondering, *If the nominative plural and genitive singular forms look the same, how do I know which is which?* That's a good question! The answer is *context*. If you see a noun that could be either nominative plural or genitive singular, you must use the context of the sentence to figure out which one it is.

Let's look at a few example sentences so you can get some practice working with the genitive case. Here's a sentence fragment to start with:

маши́на А́нны (*Anna's car* OR *the car of Anna*)

Technically speaking, the word **А́нны** could be either nominative plural or genitive singular—so you need to figure out which one it is. If it were nominative plural, this sentence fragment would mean *car Annas*, which doesn't make any grammatical sense, not to mention the fact that there is probably just one Anna, not multiple Annas. But if we interpret **А́нны** as genitive singular, then the sentence fragment means *Anna's car* and it all makes sense. This is a good example of how context can help you figure out what function a word has in a sentence. Again, a big clue here is that fact that a genitive noun usually comes right after the noun it possesses.

Here's another sentence fragment to practice with:

кни́га журнали́стки (*the female journalist's book* OR *the book of the female journalist*)

In this sentence, the word **журнали́стки** could be either nominative plural or genitive singular. So, just as in the previous example, we need to figure out which one it is. If it were nominative plural, this sentence fragment would mean *book journalists*, which doesn't make any grammatical sense. But if we interpret **журналистки** as genitive singular, then it makes much more sense because it means that the journalist is possessing the book, and the sentence fragment means *the (female) journalist's book*. Again, a genitive noun usually comes right after the noun it possesses, and that can be a signal that the noun is genitive, not nominative.

Another thing to know about the genitive case is that a noun in the genitive case can possess a noun in any other case. In other words, the noun being possessed doesn't have to be in the nominative case. Here's an example of what we mean:

Мы видим машину Екатерины. *(We see Catherine's car.)*

In that sentence, the word **машину** was the direct object and was in the accusative case. Then the word immediately following it was the genitive singular noun **Екатерины** which was possessing it. So you see, a noun in the genitive case can possess any other noun. And again, notice that the genitive noun came directly after the noun it possesses.

When you are translating from Russian to English and you see a noun in the genitive case, you must choose whether to translate it by using an apostrophe and the letter *s*, or by using the word *of*. At first, you may want to try each one and see which one sounds better. Often the context of the sentence will help you figure out which translation sounds the smoothest and most natural in English.

EXERCISES

1. **Это газета журналистки.**

2. **Меня зовут Наташа. Я покупаю машину Ольги.**

3. **Клара и актриса читают книгу Екатерины.**

4. **Женщины видят собаку актрисы.**

5. **Спортсменка читает книгу Светланы.**

6. **Журналистки видят улицу Анны.**

7. Студе́нтки чита́ют кни́гу спортсме́нки.

8. Мы не ви́дим студе́нток.

9. Э́то О́льга. Она́ покупа́ет соба́ку Кла́ры.

10. Кла́ра журнали́стка, но она́ не чита́ет газе́ты.

Answers on page 261.

LESSON 109

THE GENITIVE PLURAL

The genitive plural shows when something is being possessed by more than one person or thing. Here's an example in English:

> The girls' book.

In this example, the book belongs to more than one girl, so the apostrophe was placed after the *s* in the word *girls'*.

In Russian, the genitive plural form of a first declension feminine noun will have the zero ending. This means that for many nouns, such as **машина**, the genitive plural form will look just like the stem of the noun.

	SINGULAR	PLURAL
NOMINATIVE (SUBJECT/PRED. NOM.)	машина	машины
GENITIVE (POSSESSION)	машины	(машин)
ACCUSATIVE (DIRECT OBJECT)	машину	машины

For a noun like **женщина**, which is animate, the accusative plural form also has the zero ending. Therefore, the genitive plural and the accusative plural will look just like the stem of the noun.

	Singular	Plural
Nominative (subject/pred. nom.)	жéнщина	жéнщины
Genitive (possession)	жéнщины	жéнщин
Accusative (direct object)	жéнщину	жéнщин

But if a noun's stem ends with two consonants (as in the noun **студéнтка**) then the genitive plural form will have the zero ending, but usually with the letter **о** *(oh)* between the two consonants (more on this in the next lesson). Therefore, for an animate noun like **студéнтка**, the genitive plural will not look the same as the stem (but it will still look the same as the accusative plural).

	Singular	Plural
Nominative (subject/pred. nom.)	студéнтка	студéнтки
Genitive (possession)	студéнтки	студéнток
Accusative (direct object)	студéнтку	студéнток

Again, the genitive plural is used to show that something belongs to more than one person or thing. Let's work through some examples to help you get started working with the genitive plural. Consider the following example:

кни́га студéнток *(the book of the female students* OR *the female students' book)*

In this example, a book belongs to more than one female student. Perhaps they are sharing the book to save money (books can be expensive, you know). Anyway, because more than one female student is possessing the book, the word for *female student* is in the genitive plural. You may translate this sentence fragment as either *the book of the female students* or *the female students' book*. Both translations are technically correct, but the second one sounds a bit better and smoother. Here's another example:

Я покупа́ю маши́ну же́нщин. *(I am buying the women's car.)*

In this sentence, someone is buying a car that belongs to more than one woman. Since the car is being possessed by more than one woman, the word for *woman* is in the genitive plural. You could translate the sentence as *I am buying the car of the women,* but it would sound much smoother to translate it as *I am buying the women's car.*

EXERCISES

1. Э́то — соба́ки же́нщин.

2. Э́то маши́ны актри́с.

3. Вы ви́дите газе́ту журнали́сток.

4. Приве́т. Мы не ви́дим маши́ны студе́нток.

5. Студе́нтка чита́ет кни́гу А́нны.

6. Соба́ки же́нщины ви́дят Луну́.

7. Меня́ зову́т Ната́ша. Я актри́са.

8. Я журнали́стка, но я не чита́ю кни́ги журнали́сток.

9. Ты покупа́ешь газе́ту Кла́ры.

10. Э́то — бума́га студе́нток.

Answers on page 261.

LESSON 110

SPELLING RULE #2

So far, you only know one of the four Russian spelling rules—but that's about to change! It's time now to learn another spelling rule (don't worry, it's not too difficult).

Some sources call this rule Spelling Rule #2, and other sources call it Spelling Rule #3. Other sources call it the Five-Letter Rule. In this book we will call it Spelling Rule #2. Here it is:

> Spelling rule #2: After the letters **ж** *(zhe)*, **ч** *(cheh)*, **ш** *(shah)*, **щ** *(shsha)*, and **ц** *(tseh)*, you cannot put the vowel **о** *(oh)* if it is on an unstressed syllable. If it's an unstressed syllable, you must put a **е** *(yeh)* in place of the **о** *(oh)*.

In order to help you learn this new spelling rule, we would like to teach you a new noun: the word **де́вочка** which means *girl* (pronounced *D ᵞEH-vuch-ka*). The stem of this noun is **де́вочк-**. Here is a declension chart for this new noun. Pay special attention to the circled forms.

	Singular	Plural
Nominative (subject/pred. nom.)	де́вочка	де́вочки
Genitive (possession)	де́вочки	⬬де́вочек⬬
Accusative (direct object)	де́вочку	⬬де́вочек⬬

Did you notice anything different than usual? You already know spelling rule #1, so you know that you can't have **ы** *(y)* after a **к** *(kah)*. That's why the nominative plural and genitive singular end with **и** *(ee)* instead of **ы** *(y)*. So that's something you already know—not too unusual.

The thing we really wanted you to notice is this: In some of the nouns you know, such as **студéнтка**, noun forms with the zero ending had an **о** *(oh)* inserted before the final consonant in order to make pronunciation easier. For **студéнтка**, that gave us **студéнток** as the genitive plural and accusative plural. But for **дéвочка** things work a bit differently.

Let's experiment a bit. If we wanted to write out the noun **дéвочка** with a zero ending, we might take the stem…

дéвочк-

And then instead of adding an ending, there would be no ending at all because the zero ending is…um…no ending. So the result would look like this:

дéвочк

Then, based on what we know from other nouns such as **студéнтка**, we would add the letter **о** *(oh)* before the final consonant in order to make pronunciation easier. That would give us this:

~~дéвочок~~

Oops! That violates our new spelling rule for this lesson! Notice that in this word, the stress is on the first syllable—and according to the spelling rule, you can't put an **о** *(oh)* after **ч** *(cheh)* on an unstressed syllable. You must put a **е** *(yeh)* there instead. That would give us this:

дéвочек ☺

Now, with the letter **е** *(yeh)* there, this word obeys the Russian spelling rules and all is well. So that's the story of why the genitive plural and accusative plural forms of **дéвочка** are spelled the way they are.

In the following exercises, see if you can correctly identify and translate the various forms of **дéвочка**.

EXERCISES

1. Э́то — де́вочка.
2. Ната́ша и Светла́на де́вочки.
3. кни́га де́вочки
4. кни́га де́вочек
5. Мы ви́дим де́вочку.
6. Журнали́стка ви́дит де́вочек.
7. Они́ не ви́дят соба́ку де́вочки.
8. Де́вочки чита́ют кни́ги.
9. Де́вочки — спортсме́нки.
10. Кла́ра студе́нтка, а А́нна актри́са.

Answers on page 261.

LESSON 111

NEW WORD **ко́шка**

MEANING *cat*

PRONUNCIATION TIP: The accent is on the first syllable, so it sounds something like *KOSH-ka*.

Our new noun for this lesson is very similar to **де́вочка**, our new word from last lesson, because both words are animate and both must obey the same spelling rules.

The stem of this noun is **ко́шк-** so it must obey spelling rule #1, that you can't have a **ы** *(y)* after a **к** *(kah)*. Also, notice that since a cat is animate, the genitive plural and accusative plural forms have the zero ending. Finally, notice that because of spelling rule #2, an **е** *(yeh)* is inserted before the final consonant instead of an **о** *(oh)*.

	Singular	Plural
Nominative (subject/pred. nom.)	ко́шка	ко́шки
Genitive (possession)	ко́шки	ко́шек
Accusative (direct object)	ко́шку	ко́шек

EXERCISES

1. Э́то ко́шка.

2. Э́то ко́шки.

3. Э́то ко́шка де́вочки.

4. Соба́ка ви́дит ко́шку О́льги.

5. Ты не соба́ка. Ты ко́шка!

6. Ко́шка ви́дит де́вочку.

7. Соба́ка де́вочки ви́дит ко́шку.

8. Де́вочки чита́ют кни́гу спортсме́нок.

9. Же́нщины студе́нтки. Они́ не актри́сы.

10. Де́вочки ви́дят соба́ку, но они́ не ви́дят ко́шку.

Answers on page 261.

LESSON 112

NEW WORD   **ба́бушка**

MEANING   *grandmother*

PRONUNCIATION TIP: You may have heard this Russian word before, but pronounced incorrectly with the stress on the second syllable: *ba-BOOSH-ka*. Instead, notice that the stress is really on the first syllable, so it sounds like *BAH-boosh-ka*.

The stem of this noun is **бабушк-** so it must obey spelling rule #1. Also, notice that since a grandmother is animate, the genitive plural and accusative plural forms have the zero ending. Finally, notice that because of spelling rule #2, an **e** *(yeh)* is inserted before the final consonant instead of an **o** *(oh)*.

	Singular	Plural
Nominative (subject/pred. nom.)	бáбушка	бáбушки
Genitive (possession)	бáбушки	бáбушек
Accusative (direct object)	бáбушку	бáбушек

EXERCISES

1. Э́то — кóшка бáбушки.

2. Натáша — бáбушка А́нны.

3. Бáбушка вѝдит дéвочек, но дéвочки не вѝдят бáбушку.

4. Кóшка дéвочки вѝдит собáку.

5. Журналѝстка покупáет кóшку.

6. Кóшки дéвочек вѝдят собáк.

7. Менá зовýт Светлáна. Я спортсмéнка и студéнтка.

8. Кóшка не читáет газéту!

9. Вы не вѝдите кóшку.

10. Э́то не собáка!

Answers on page 262.

LESSON 113

NEW WORD   **ру́чка**

MEANING   *pen*

PRONUNCIATION TIP: The letter **ч** *(cheh)* has a *ch* sound, so this word sounds something like *ROOCH-ka*.

Our new word for this lesson means *pen*, as in the kind of pen you write with. It's related to the Russian word for *hand* which is **рука́**.

Examine the chart below as you consider the characteristics of **ру́чка**. The stem of the noun is **ру́чк-**. Since the last letter of the stem is **к** *(kah)*, the nominative plural ending cannot be **ы** *(y)* because of spelling rule #1. Therefore the nominative plural ending is **и** *(ee)*. This noun is inanimate, so the accusative plural form does not have the zero ending. Instead, it looks identical to the nominative plural form. Finally, notice that the genitive plural form does have the zero ending, but the vowel that gets inserted before the final consonant is the letter **е** *(yeh)* due to spelling rule #2.

	Singular	Plural
Nominative (subject/pred. nom.)	ру́чка	ру́чки
Genitive (possession)	ру́чки	ру́чек
Accusative (direct object)	ру́чку	ру́чки

EXERCISES

1. Э́то ру́чки де́вочек.

2. Э́то ру́чка журнали́стки.

3. Мы не ви́дим ру́чки Ната́ши.

4. Вы чита́ете кни́гу Екатери́ны.

5. Э́то студе́нтки. Они́ чита́ют газе́ты журнали́сток.

6. Спаси́бо, О́льга. Меня́ зову́т А́нна.

7. Кла́ра и Екатери́на покупа́ют газе́ты де́вочки.

8. Э́то соба́ка Кла́ры. Кла́ра — студе́нтка.

9. Я ба́бушка, а ты спортсме́нка.

10. Я журнали́стка, но я не чита́ю кни́ги.

Answers on page 262.

LESSON 114

NEW WORD **еда́**

MEANING *food*

PRONUNCIATION TIP: The letter **е** *(yeh)* is unstressed in this word, so it will have a reduced vowel sound. Therefore this word sounds something like *yi-DAH*.

In Russian the word **еда́** is singular only because it is considered to be something that you cannot count. It's sort of like the word *rice* in English. You can have a small amount of rice, a large amount of rice, or no rice at all. But you can't have one rice or two rice. You can use this new word the same way you would use the word *food* in English.

Nominative (subject/pred. nom.)	еда́
Genitive (possession)	еды́
Accusative (direct object)	еду́

EXERCISES

1. **Э́то еда́ де́вочки.**

2. **Э́то еда́ соба́ки.**

3. **Э́то еда́ соба́к.**

4. **Ко́шка ви́дит еду́ Светла́ны.**

5. Мы покупа́ем еду́, а вы покупа́ете кни́ги.

6. Ба́бушка покупа́ет еду́, а де́вочки покупа́ют газе́ты.

7. Же́нщина ви́дит ру́чки, но она́ не ви́дит кни́ги.

8. Мы не чита́ем кни́гу спортсме́нок.

9. Приве́т, Екатери́на и Ната́ша!

10. Э́то не маши́на Кла́ры. Э́то маши́на А́нны.

Answers on page 262.

LESSON 115

NEW WORD   **я даю́**

MEANING   *I give, I am giving*

PRONUNCIATION TIP: Notice that for all the different forms of this verb, the accent is on the verb's personal ending. Therefore **даю́** sounds something like *da-YOO*. Most of the other forms of this verb contain the letter **ё** *(yo)* which has an *o* sound. Therefore a form like **даёшь** would sound like *die-YOSH*.

Way back in lesson 30, we told you about the letter **ё** *(yo)*. We told you that it was relatively rare, but that you would eventually see it again in this book. And now, that time has finally arrived!

In lesson 92, we mentioned that when it comes to personal verb endings, the consonants at the ends of the endings tend to stay the same, but the vowels change. And that is what is happening here. Notice that four out of the six present tense forms of this new verb contain the letter **ё** *(yo)*.

	Singular	Plural
First Person	я даю́	мы даём
Second Person	ты даёшь	вы даёте
Third Person	он/она́ даёт	они́ даю́т

Again, four of these personal endings begin with the letter **ё** *(yo)*. This vowel is always stressed, so the stress will automatically fall on that syllable. And because this letter is always stressed, there is no need to indicate the stress with an accent mark. An accent mark would be redundant—and repetitive—and it would say the same thing twice.

In this book, we will always indicate the letter **ё** *(yo)* by using the two dots over it. That is the "correct" way to display this letter. But out there in the real world, in newspapers and on the internet, the two dots over the letter **ё** *(yo)* are often omitted. In that kind of situation, it will look like the letter **e** *(yeh)*, but it's really still the letter **ё** *(yo)*. Even without the dots, native Russian speakers just know when it's a **ё** *(yo)*.

In the following exercises, we have given you a few incomplete or fragmentary sentences. Soon, we will teach you the additional grammar you need for more complete sentences about giving things to people, but for now just practice with these less-than-perfect sentences.

EXERCISES

1. **Я даю́ еду́.**
2. **Вы даёте кни́гу.**
3. **Он даёт ру́чку.**
4. **Ба́бушка даёт газе́ту.**
5. **Мы даём кни́ги и ру́чки.**
6. **Вы даёте маши́ну.**
7. **Они́ даю́т еду́.**
8. **Э́то еда́ ко́шки.**
9. **Э́то кни́ги де́вочек.**
10. **Вы ви́дите студе́нток, а мы не ви́дим студе́нток.**

Answers on page 262.

LESSON 116

INDIRECT OBJECTS

You already know what a direct object is—it's the target of the action being performed by the subject of the sentence. In this lesson we want to teach you about a secondary target of the action called an *indirect object*. The indirect object is the party in the sentence that is receiving or benefiting. In English, indirect objects are often accompanied by the words *to* or *for*. In each of the following examples, the indirect object is underlined:

- He gave the book to Johnny.
- She told a story to the class.
- She bought some presents for her friends.
- He showed his rock collection to Mr. Green.

And now, the same sentences but with a different word order:

- He gave Johnny the book.
- She told the class a story.
- She bought her friends some presents.
- He showed Mr. Green his rock collection.

So, although these two ways of expressing the indirect object are worded differently, they still mean the same thing.

By the way, take care not to confuse indirect objects with objects of the preposition. Consider the following example:

I sailed to the island.

In this example the word *to* is just a preposition, not part of an indirect object (more about prepositions later).

In the following exercises, see if you can identify the direct object and the indirect object.

EXERCISES

1. I loaned the money to my friend.
2. We donated money to the charity.
3. He showed the class an example.
4. Let's get some tea for Mom.
5. Henry bought a gift for his teacher.
6. They made us some sandwiches.
7. He told the judge his story.
8. The band played another song for the audience.
9. I brought copies for everyone.
10. My mother bought me a shirt.

Answers on page 263.

LESSON 117

THE DATIVE CASE

In Russian, we indicate the indirect object in a sentence by using a noun case called the *dative case*. On the chart, this is the third of the six cases. For the feminine nouns we are studying in this book, the ending of the noun changes to **-e** in the dative singular.

In English, depending on word order, we sometimes need a preposition such as *to* or *for* to indicate what the indirect object is. For example, the following sentences express the same idea, but the second sentence requires a preposition:

- I am giving *the boy* a book.
- I am giving a book *to the boy*.

But in Russian, the dative case shows what the indirect object is without the help of any preposition. The idea of *to* or *for* is embedded or included in the basic meaning of the dative case, so an extra Russian preposition is not needed. This is a big difference between English and Russian that you will have to keep in mind as you translate.

Observe the dative case in the chart below:

	Singular	Plural
Nominative (subject/pred. nom.)	же́нщина	же́нщины
Genitive (possession)	же́нщины	же́нщин
Dative (ind. obj./obj. of prep.)	же́нщине	
Accusative (direct object)	же́нщину	же́нщин

As we mentioned before, the indirect object in a sentence is the party that is benefiting or receiving. We have made a few sentences with **я даю́**, like this:

Я даю́ кни́гу. *(I am giving the/a book.)*

But that's not really a very good sentence because it's incomplete—we know who is giving the book, but who is its recipient? Don't worry—now that you know the dative case, we can use it to indicate the party that is benefiting or receiving, like this:

Я даю́ кни́гу <u>же́нщине</u>. *(I am giving the/a book <u>to the/a woman</u>.)*

In that sentence the word *woman* was the indirect object because she was the recipient of the book. Therefore, in order to show this, the word *woman* was put into the dative case. When translating the dative noun **же́нщине** into English, we can translate it as *to the/a woman*. Again, even though there is no Russian word for *to* in the sentence, the idea of *to* is embedded in the meaning of the dative case. Therefore in order to translate the dative case accurately, we need to include extra words such as *to* or *for* in our English translations.

EXERCISES

1. **Студе́нтки даю́т еду́ ко́шке.**
2. **Светла́на даёт ру́чку де́вочке.**
3. **Мы даём кни́гу студе́нтке.**
4. **Ты не даёшь бума́гу же́нщине.**
5. **Вы даёте ру́чки актри́се.**
6. **Спортсме́нки чита́ют газе́ты.**
7. **Э́то ру́чки журнали́сток.**
8. **Я не даю́ газе́ту Светла́не. Она́ не журнали́стка.**
9. **Э́то ко́шка де́вочки.**
10. **Соба́ка О́льги ви́дит ко́шек.**

Answers on page 263.

LESSON 118

THE DATIVE PLURAL

In the last lesson, we saw examples of indirect objects in Russian that were singular. These indirect objects were in the dative singular, and the ending was **-е.**

But if the party that is receiving or benefiting is made up of more than one person or thing, that indirect object will need to be in the dative plural. For the feminine nouns we are studying in this book, the dative plural is formed by adding **-ам** to the stem of the noun.

Here is an example of a plural indirect object which is represented by a noun in the dative plural:

Мы даём еду́ же́нщинам. *(We are giving food to the women.)*

In that sentence, someone is giving food to a group of women. Since the women are receiving or benefiting, the word *women* is the indirect object. Therefore, in the Russian sentence, the word for *women* is put into the dative plural.

	Singular	Plural
Nominative (subject/pred. nom.)	же́нщина	же́нщины
Genitive (possession)	же́нщины	же́нщин
Dative (ind. obj./obj. of prep.)	же́нщине	(же́нщинам)
Accusative (direct object)	же́нщину	же́нщин

EXERCISES

1. Екатери́на даёт ру́чки журнали́сткам.
2. Он даёт еду́ соба́кам и ко́шкам.
3. Я даю́ ру́чку Кла́ры А́нне.
4. Ба́бушка даёт кни́ги де́вочкам.
5. Мы даём соба́к Екатери́не.
6. Же́нщины даю́т еду́ студе́нтке.
7. Э́то Светла́на. Она́ даёт еду́ ко́шкам.
8. Он не покупа́ет газе́ту. Он покупа́ет кни́гу.
9. Э́то еда́ соба́ки.
10. Я соба́ка, а ты ко́шка.

Answers on page 263.

LESSON 119

NEW WORD **я пока́зываю**

MEANING *I show, I am showing*

PRONUNCIATION TIP: Since the accent is on the second syllable, the word **пока́зываю** sounds something like *puh-KAH-zy-va-yoo*.

	Singular	Plural
First Person	я пока́зываю	мы пока́зываем
Second Person	ты пока́зываешь	вы пока́зываете
Third Person	он/она́ пока́зывает	они́ пока́зывают

This verb is longer than the others you have learned, but notice that the endings are exactly the same as those you have seen with other verbs like **чита́ю** (*I read*). The verb stem has four syllables (**пока́зыва-**), but the verb behaves perfectly normally.

With this verb you can make sentences in which someone is showing something to someone. In a sentence like that, the thing that is being shown will be in the accusative case, and the party that the thing is being shown to will be in the dative case.

Here are a couple of examples of this kind of sentence:

- **Кла́ра пока́зывает бума́гу Екатери́не.** *(Clara is showing the paper to Catherine.)*
- **Журнали́стка пока́зывает кни́ги студе́нткам.** *(The (female) journalist is showing (the) books to the (female) students.)*

EXERCISES

1. Она́ пока́зывает еду́ соба́ке.

2. Актри́са пока́зывает кни́гу журнали́сткам.

3. Де́вочка пока́зывает соба́ку спортсме́нке.

4. Ты пока́зываешь маши́ну актри́сы же́нщинам.

5. Вы пока́зываете еду́ ко́шкам.

6. Он пока́зывает еду́ соба́кам, но он не даёт еду́ собака́м.

7. Мы пока́зываем ру́чку журнали́стке.

8. Я даю́ бума́гу Кла́ре.

9. Вы чита́ете кни́гу ба́бушки.

10. Соба́ка ви́дит еду́ А́нны!

Answers on page 263.

LESSON 120

RUSSIAN WORD ORDER CAN BE FLEXIBLE

As a speaker of English, you are accustomed to putting the words in your sentences in a certain order. In some languages (like English), the order of words is not very flexible because the order of the words helps communicate the meaning of the sentence. But in other languages, the word order is much more flexible—you can mix up the words in almost any order and the sentence will still say the same thing!

In Russian, there are certain expectations for what order the words ought to be in. But there is still some flexibility to Russian word order. This is largely because of the various endings that nouns can have. In Russian, the form (ending) of a noun shows what that noun is doing no matter where it is in the sentence. But in English, that's not true.

Here's an example of what we mean—observe the subject and direct object in the following English sentence:

Clara sees Anna.

In that sentence, we know that Clara is the subject of the sentence and Anna is the direct object because of the word order. If we switched the places of the two names, here is what would happen:

Anna sees Clara.

Now, because of the change in word order, Anna is the subject and Clara is the direct object. In English, when you change the word order of a sentence, it can really change the meaning!

Now let's compare how that same word order change might affect a Russian sentence. Here's our original sentence, but this time in Russian.

Кла́ра ви́дит А́нну.

Just by looking at this sentence you can tell that Clara's name is in the nominative case while Anna's name is in the accusative case. This means that Anna must be the direct object in this sentence. Now let's flip the word order like before.

Áнну видит Клáра.

This word order is less common, but it is still correct Russian. Now Anna's name is the first word of the sentence...does that mean it's the subject of the sentence? No! It's still in the accusative case, so it cannot be the subject. Furthermore, Clara's name is still in the nominative case, so it can't be the direct object. The direct object must be in the accusative case. Therefore even though we have changed the word order, the endings of the nouns are the same, and so the sentence means the same thing as before. Changing the word order did not change the meaning. But in the corresponding English sentence, changing the word order did change the meaning because we don't have those special noun endings.

So here's our point: Because Russian nouns have special endings that show what they are doing in a sentence, Russian word order is much more flexible than English word order. So when you read a Russian sentence, you must pay careful attention to the endings of the various nouns (and verbs, too) so that you know what the sentence is communicating, regardless of the order the words are in.

LESSON 121

FLEXIBLE WORD ORDER IN ACTION!

In the last lesson, we took a break from learning new words so that we could talk about the flexibility of word order in Russian. We used a fairly unusual Russian sentence to demonstrate the concept of flexible word order—a sentence in which we had swapped the placement of the subject and direct object. In this book you won't see any changes in word order that are as drastic as that sentence, but we do want to begin to introduce you to some of the more subtle variations in word order that you might commonly see in Russian sentences.

The part of the sentence we want to discuss here is the part near the end where the direct object and indirect object are. Observe this sentence:

Я даю́ газе́ту Кла́ре. *(I am giving the/a newspaper to Clara* OR *I am giving Clara the/a newspaper.)*

In that sentence the word **газе́ту** is the direct object and the word **Кла́ре** is the indirect object. Notice that the indirect object here is coming after the direct object. This is the word order we have been using ever since you learned about indirect objects.

But here's the new thing we want to tell you: the indirect object doesn't have to come after the direct object. It can be placed before it, too, like this:

Я даю́ Кла́ре газе́ту. *(I am giving the/a newspaper to Clara* OR *I am giving Clara the/a newspaper.)*

Even though the word order has changed, the sentence still means exactly the same thing! So from now on, don't expect the indirect object to automatically come after the direct object every time—you need to watch the endings of the nouns carefully so you can tell which ones are direct objects and which ones are indirect objects. Don't assume that the word order will tell you what the sentence means!

LESSON 122

NEW WORD **су́мка**

MEANING *purse, handbag*

PRONUNCIATION TIP: The word **су́мка** sounds something like *SOOM-ka*.

Notice that the **к** *(kah)* at the end of the stem means that the genitive singular and nominative plural endings will follow spelling rule #1.

	Singular	Plural
Nominative (subject/pred. nom.)	су́мка	су́мки
Genitive (possession)	су́мки	су́мок
Dative (ind. obj./obj. of prep.)	су́мке	су́мкам
Accusative (direct object)	су́мку	су́мки

EXERCISES

1. Э́то су́мка Екатери́ны.

2. Мы пока́зываем су́мку О́льге и Ната́ше.

3. Же́нщина пока́зыает актри́сам су́мки.

4. Э́то су́мки студе́нток.

5. Журнали́стка даёт ру́чку студе́нтке.

6. Вы читáете газéту Клáры.

7. Óльга и Екатерина даю́т собáкам еду́.

8. Он не покупáет книги. Он покупáет еду́.

9. Я покáзываю книгу Натáше, но я не даю́ книгу Натáше.

10. Э́то бáбушка Клáры.

Answers on page 264.

LESSON 123

PRONOUNS CAN HAVE CASES, TOO

In this book, we have spent lots of time learning that nouns can be in different cases. But did you know that pronouns can be in different cases, too?

Take, for example, the word **я** which means *I*. You may not have realized it yet, but this particular pronoun has a case just like nouns do. This particular pronoun is nominative, which means that it can only be either the subject of a sentence or a predicate nominative. The situation is the same way in English. Consider this sentence:

> I see Bob.

In that sentence, the subject is *I* and the direct object is *Bob*. In English, the pronoun *I* is nominative, so it works fine as the subject of the sentence. But since *I* is nominative, it can't be the direct object in a sentence. In other words, you can't say this:

> Bob sees I.

In that sentence, you can't use *I* in that particular spot because that word is the direct object. So instead of *I*, you have to say *me*, like this.

> Bob sees me.

Again, in Russian, the pronoun **я** is nominative. This means that it can only be the subject or predicate nominative in a sentence. Therefore if you want to have **я** as a genitive, dative, or accusative, you have to use different words for those.

You already know the accusative form of this pronoun—remember this phrase?

Меня́ зову́т А́нна. *(My name is Anna.)*

The word **меня́** is the accusative form of **я**, so it translates into English as *me* (remember that the phrase **Меня́ зову́т А́нна** literally says *They call me Anna*).

You don't know the dative form yet—so in this lesson, let's learn the dative form of **я** which is **мне**. This word sounds something like *mnʸeh*, and it can mean things like *to me* or *for me*.

Let's take the three pronouns we have talked about in this lesson and put them into a declension chart:

Nominative (subject/pred. nom.)	**я**
Dative (ind. obj./obj. of prep.)	**мне**
Accusative (direct object)	**меня́**

Here's an example of how you can use our new dative pronoun in a sentence:

> **Он даёт мне кни́гу.** *(He is giving me the/a book* OR *He is giving the /a book to me.)*

In that sentence, **мне** is in the dative case because it is the indirect object.

You already know how to use the word **меня́** in the phrase **Меня́ зову́т…** But here's something new you can do with it—use it as a direct object in a sentence, like this:

> **Ната́ша ви́дит меня́.** *(Natasha sees me.)*

Now that you know the dative and accusative forms of **я**, we can make slightly more interesting sentences!

EXERCISES

1. Áнна пока́зывает мне маши́ны.
2. Она́ меня́ ви́дит.
3. Де́вочка даёт мне су́мку.
4. Соба́ки меня́ не ви́дят.
5. Ба́бушка А́нны даёт еду́ де́вочкам.
6. Ко́шка де́вочки ви́дит еду́.
7. Э́то еда́ Кла́ры. Э́то не еда́ соба́ки.
8. Же́нщина — актри́са.
9. Вы даёте кни́гу Ната́ше.
10. Они́ пока́зывают соба́ку О́льге.

Answers on page 264.

LESSON 124

MORE ABOUT WORD ORDER

A few lessons ago we took some time to tell you that word order in Russian can be flexible. Now we want to show you how the word order can vary with the pronouns you know.

In the last lesson, we worked with sentences like the ones below, with the dative and accusative forms of **я**:

- **Де́вочка даёт мне еду́.** *(The girl is giving me (the) food* OR *The girl is giving (the) food to me.)*
- **Ко́шка ви́дит меня́.** *(The cat sees me.)*

In those sentences we use an English-sounding word order to help you learn—but the reality is that in Russian, sentences like these could have several different word orders. Therefore, you might encounter a Russian sentence that has the same word order you might see in an English sentence, like this:

Ната́ша ви́дит меня́. *(Natasha sees me.)*

Or you might see a sentence that puts the direct object before the verb, like this:

Ната́ша меня́ ви́дит.

A word-for-word translation of that example would say *Natasha me sees*. But of course, when you translate that kind of sentence into English, you would rearrange the words into a natural-sounding English word order. Therefore, you would translate the example sentence seen above as *Natasha sees me*.

And the same thing is true for indirect objects. You may encounter a Russian sentence with an English-sounding word order, like this:

Он даёт мне кни́гу. *(He is giving me the/a book* OR *He is giving the /a book to me.)*

Or, you might see this order, with the indirect object placed before the verb, like this:

Он мне даёт кни́гу.

A word-for-word translation of that example would say *He to me is giving the book*. But of course, when you translate that kind of sentence into English, you would rearrange the words into a natural-sounding English word order. Therefore, you would translate the example sentence seen above as *He is giving me the book* OR *He is giving the book to me*.

One last thing—a native Russian speaker can change around the word order depending on what that person wants to emphasize. A native speaker may also pronounce a certain word with more stress or volume, just as we often do in English for emphasis. In fact, the pitch of a native Russian speaker's voice can rise and fall dramatically within a sentence, depending on what the speaker wants to communicate. So as you continue to study Russian, watch out for variation in the way people express themselves, both in spoken and written Russian.

But as far as written Russian goes, the big point we want to make in this lesson is that you cannot expect a Russian sentence to have English word order. In other words, you can't make assumptions about the meaning of a Russian sentence based on the word order. Instead, you have to consider each word individually, carefully observing each noun's case endings. What role does each individual noun play? Is it dative? Is it accusative? Since you cannot depend on word order to show you what the relationships are between the words, you must use your knowledge of noun cases to determine how the words are working together to create meaningful sentences.

LESSON 125

NEW WORD **библиотéка**

MEANING *library*

PRONUNCIATION TIP: The word **библиотéка** has the stress on the fourth syllable, so it sounds something like *beeb-lee-a-TʸEK-uh*.

The word *bibliotheca* (or something very similar) is the word for *library* in many European languages such as Latin, Dutch, Portuguese, Spanish, and Italian.

This new word is significant because it is the first word you have learned for a place. Soon we will be able to make more complicated sentences in which people are going places. In the meantime, head over to the library and "check out" this declension chart:

	Singular	Plural
Nominative (subject/pred. nom.)	библиотéка	библиотéки
Genitive (possession)	библиотéки	библиотéк
Dative (ind. obj./obj. of prep.)	библиотéке	библиотéкам
Accusative (direct object)	библиотéку	библиотéки

EXERCISES

1. Ната́ша пока́зывает библиоте́ку студе́нткам.
2. Мы даём кни́ги библиоте́ке.
3. Екатери́на даёт мне кни́гу.
4. Э́то не кни́ги библиоте́к.
5. Актри́са меня́ ви́дит!
6. Журнали́стка даёт мне кни́гу.
7. Э́то кни́га библиоте́ки.
8. Они́ покупа́ют еду́, а мы покупа́ем су́мки.
9. Же́нщина пока́зывает мне су́мку, но я не покупа́ю су́мку.
10. Вы даёте студе́нткам бума́гу.

Answers on page 264.

LESSON 126

HOW TO SAY THAT YOU LIKE SOMETHING

In everyday conversation, we are constantly saying that we like or dislike certain things. Now it is time for you to learn how to say this kind of thing in Russian.

But it's a little complicated. In Russian, when you say you like something, the sentence structure is different than it would be in English. Let's compare the structure of this type of sentence in English and in Russian. Here is how you would say this kind of thing in English:

> I like the book.

In that sentence, the subject is the word *I*, and the word *like* is the verb. The word *book* is the direct object.

Now let's take a look at how that same sentence would be structured in Russian:

> The book is pleasing to me.

That's the general idea, although an exact, word-for-word translation of how you would say it in Russian reads like this:

> To me is pleasing the book.

As you can see, in this sentence, everything is reversed. The word *book* is now the subject of the sentence instead of being the direct object. Likewise, instead of the speaker being the subject, the speaker *(me)* is the one being pleased by the book. And the verb is not to *like*, but to *be pleasing*.

Compare these two sentence structures until you understand them well, and then go on to the next lesson.

LESSON 127

I LIKE IT! I LIKE IT!

In the last lesson, we learned that in English you would say *I like the book*, but in Russian you would literally say *To me is pleasing the book.* Now let's learn how to say this sentence in Russian.

In order to do that, we need to learn the Russian verb that means *to be pleasing*. Let's examine the following chart:

	SINGULAR	PLURAL
FIRST PERSON	(unnecessary)	(unnecessary)
SECOND PERSON	(unnecessary)	(unnecessary)
THIRD PERSON	**нра́вится**	**нра́вятся**

These verb forms look different from the verbs you know so far because they have a special ending. It's a long story, but a certain category of verbs (reflexives) takes the special ending **-ся**. But the point we really want you to see is that without this special ending, these verb forms would look relatively normal to you: **нра́вит** and **нра́вят**. So these verbs aren't as unusual as they look.

The only forms of this verb that we will study in this book are the third person singular and the third person plural. The third person singular form **нра́вится** means *he is pleasing, she is pleasing,* or *it is pleasing.*

Notice that at the beginning of this word there is an *n* sound right next to an *r* sound, so the first syllable sounds like *nra*. The ending of this word is one that happens frequently with Russian verbs. The **тся** combination looks like it should be palatalized, but Russian speakers say this syllable so fast that the palatalization does not really happen, and so it ends up sounding like *tsuh*. Therefore, the word as a whole sounds something like *NRA-vee-tsuh*.

The third person plural form **нра́вятся** means *they are pleasing*. It sounds similar to the third person singular form, but the middle part of the word is different. It sounds something like *NRA-vya-tsuh*.

These two verbs sound so much alike that you may have trouble distinguishing them from one another when you hear them—but in written format you'll be able to tell them apart because you can see the way they are spelled. The singular one has the letter **и** *(ee)* and the plural one has the letter **я** *(ya)*.

So, if you like one book, you would use the third person singular form, like this:

Нра́вится кни́га. *(The book is pleasing.)*

And if you like more than one book, you would use the third person plural form, like this:

Нра́вятся кни́ги. *(The books are pleasing.)*

A quick reminder: in English, when you like something, the thing that you like is the direct object. But in a Russian sentence, the structure is different, and the thing you like is really the subject of the sentence, so it will be in the nominative case. That's why, in the example sentences above, the words **кни́га** and **кни́ги** are both nominative.

Now we need to figure out how to say *to me* in Russian. You already know this word: it's **мне**, which is the dative form of **я**.

Now let's put it all together and try to make the full sentence.

Мне нра́вится кни́га.

An exact, word-for-word translation would say *To me is pleasing the book*. But we will translate it into English as *I like the book*. Here's that same sentence, but with the subject and verb plural instead of singular.

Мне нра́вятся кни́ги.

An exact, word-for-word translation would say *To me are pleasing the books* but we will translate it into English as *I like the books*. Or, it could be someone saying that they like books in general, so it could be translated as *I like books*.

EXERCISES

1. Мне нра́вятся ко́шки.
2. Мне нра́вится су́мка.
3. Мне нра́вятся библиоте́ки и кни́ги.
4. Же́нщина пока́зывает су́мку Екатери́не.
5. Ба́бушка Екатери́ны даёт еду́ ко́шке.
6. Светла́на — ба́бушка Ната́ши.
7. Они́ ви́дят соба́ку де́вочки.
8. Э́то ру́чка О́льги.
9. Он даёт ко́шку Кла́ре.
10. Ты даёшь студе́нткам ру́чки.

Answers on page 264.

LESSON 128

I DON'T LIKE IT!

In the last lesson, you learned how to say that you like something in Russian. Now let's learn how to say that you *don't* like something.

All you have to do is throw in the word **не**, which means *not*. So if you have a sentence like this…

Мне нра́вится кни́га. *(To me is pleasing the book.)*

…you would take the word **не** and park it just before the verb, like this:

Мне не нра́вится кни́га. *(To me not is pleasing the book.)*

Of course, this word order is completely different from English. In English, the sentence "To me not is pleasing the book" is just a jumble of words that doesn't make any sense. We are only showing you this literal translation so that you can see how the sentence structure works in Russian. The way that kind of sentence really would be translated into English is *I do not like the book*.

EXERCISES

1. **Мне нра́вятся кни́ги, но мне не нра́вятся библиоте́ки.**
2. **Же́нщина пока́зывает мне су́мку, но мне не нра́вится су́мка.**
3. **Соба́ка Светла́ны меня́ ви́дит. Мне не нра́вится соба́ка Светла́ны.**
4. **Они́ актри́су ви́дят.**
5. **Ба́бушка О́льги даёт мне еду́.**
6. **Меня́ зову́т Кла́ра. Мне нра́вятся ко́шки.**

7. Вы даёте кни́гу Екатери́ны Ната́ше.

8. Ты — не ко́шка. Ты — соба́ка.

9. Мы пока́зываем же́нщинам су́мки.

10. Он даёт ру́чки студе́нткам.

Answers on page 265.

LESSON 129

ANYBODY CAN LIKE SOMETHING!

By now you have a bit of experience working with sentences that say *I like* or *I don't like*. In order to make those sentences, we take either the third person singular verb **нра́вится** or the third person plural verb **нра́вятся** and we use it with the dative pronoun **мне**.

The new thing we want to tell you in this lesson is that you can make this kind of statement with any noun in the dative case. It's easy to do—just take the person or animal that is liking something, put his or her name in the dative case, and park it at the beginning of the sentence. In this example, Anna likes a book:

А́нне нра́вится кни́га. *(To Anna is pleasing the book.)*

In that example, the book is pleasing—but instead of **мне** in the dative case, we have Anna's name in the dative case, so the book is pleasing to Anna. Therefore we would translate this sentence into English as *Anna likes the book*.

In order to make a sentence about multiple people or animals liking something (or not liking something), just use the dative plural, like this:

Соба́кам нра́вится еда́. *(To the dogs is pleasing the food.)*

In that example, the food is pleasing, and since the word for *dogs* is in the dative plural, the dogs are the ones to whom the food is pleasing. Therefore we would translate this sentence into English as *The dogs like (the) food*.

So now we can have exercises in which any animate being, whether person or animal, can like or dislike something. You're really making progress with your Russian skills, so keep up the good work!

EXERCISES

1. Соба́кам не нра́вится же́нщина.
2. Светла́не нра́вится су́мка, но Ната́ше не нра́вится су́мка.
3. Актри́сам нра́вятся маши́ны.
4. Студе́нткам нра́вятся библиоте́ки.
5. Соба́ке нра́вятся ко́шки.
6. Соба́ке нра́вится де́вочка.
7. Мне нра́вятся соба́ки, а Екатери́не нра́вятся ко́шки.
8. Ко́шке нра́вится маши́на.
9. Же́нщина даёт еду́ ко́шкам, но ко́шкам не нра́вится еда́.
10. Соба́ке не нра́вится ко́шка!

Answers on page 265.

LESSON 130

PREPOSITIONS

A *preposition* is a word that shows a relationship or connection between two nouns. Examples of prepositions are *in, to, from, below, above,* and *beside.* Here's an example of a sentence with a preposition.

    The bicycle is inside the garage.

In that sentence, the word *inside* is a preposition. Notice that in this sentence there are two items being talked about: the bicycle and the garage. The preposition showed the relationship between the two items.

The person saying this sentence wants to tell someone about the location of the bicycle. There are several ways to tell someone the location of an item. The speaker could have indicated the location of the bicycle a different way. If the bicycle happened to be nearby, the speaker could have simply pointed at it and said, "It's over here," or "It's over there." But with a preposition, you don't have to be near the object you want to talk about—you can use words to indicate its location by using something else as a point of reference. You can use prepositions to talk about relationships in space, time, or when referring to abstract concepts.

Let's look at that sentence again and observe how the speaker used the garage as a way to specify the location of the bicycle.

    The bicycle is inside the garage.

The speaker used the garage as a point of reference to show where the bicycle was. The preposition *inside* referred directly to the garage. In grammatical terms, the word that the preposition refers to is called the *object of the preposition.*

Therefore, in this sentence, the word *inside* is the preposition and the word *garage* is the object of the preposition.

Just for practice, in each of the following sentences, see if you can spot the preposition and the object of the preposition.

EXERCISES

1. Your book fell behind the couch.
2. Just put that plant beside the lamp.
3. The spare tire is in the trunk.
4. We drove through the tunnel.
5. I just saw a chipmunk run under the house!
6. I want to get this done before lunch.
7. After school, the accordion ensemble will rehearse again.
8. The new store is by the post office.
9. You aren't allowed to do that on campus.
10. Have you ever wondered what is beyond that mountain?

Answers on page 265.

LESSON 131

THE PREPOSITIONAL CASE

Now that you are learning about prepositions, it's time to learn about the sixth of the six Russian noun cases, which is called the *prepositional case*. The prepositional case is (as the name suggests) used with prepositions. Mainly, this case is used as the object of the Russian prepositions that mean *in* and *at*.

In the chart below, study the prepositional singular form of **библиотéка**. Notice that the prepositional singular ending (**-e**) is the same as the dative singular ending.

	Singular	Plural
Nominative (subject/pred. nom.)	библиотéка	библиотéки
Genitive (possession)	библиотéки	библиотéк
Dative (ind. obj./obj. of prep.)	библиотéке	библиотéкам
Accusative (direct object)	библиотéку	библиотéки
Prepositional (object of prep.)	**библиотéке**	

And now that you know the prepositional case, you need to learn a preposition to use it with. Below is the Russian preposition that means *at* (or sometimes *in*). It consists of only one letter.

в

At first glance, you might think that this short word would be pronounced *vuh*—but unfortunately it's not that simple. In print, this preposition is separate, and there is a space between it and the next word, so it will be easy to recognize. But in spoken Russian, this preposition is pronounced as if it is joined to the next word. Sometimes it will sound like a quick *v* sound at the beginning of the next word, and other times it will sound like a quick *f* sound. The pronunciation of **в** depends on the kind of sound that the next word starts with—whether or not the first sound of the next word is a sound that is pronounced with the vocal cords vibrating.

Here's what we mean: with some sounds, the speaker's vocal cords vibrate during the production of the sound. Here's a fun way to experience this for yourself: as you pronounce the words below, gently rest your fingers on the front of your throat. As you pronounce the underlined portion of each word, you should feel that your vocal cords are vibrating.

- <u>v</u>elvet
- <u>m</u>arvelous
- <u>a</u>ble

But when you pronounce the underlined portion of the words below, you should feel that your vocal cords are *not* vibrating.

- <u>f</u>rog
- <u>s</u>ardines
- <u>th</u>ink

See the difference? These different pronunciations have special names or terms associated with them. Sounds that are pronounced with the vocal cords vibrating are called *voiced* sounds, and sounds that are pronounced without the vocal cords vibrating are called *voiceless* sounds.

So again, the pronunciation of **в** depends on whether the next word starts with a voiced sound or a voiceless sound. If the next word starts with a voiceless sound, **в** will also be voiceless and so it will sound like an *f*. But if the next word starts with a voiced sound, **в** will also be voiced and it will sound like a *v*.

You can use the preposition **в** along with the prepositional case to say that something or someone is "at" someplace. Here is an example:

в библиотéке *(at the library)*

In that example, the preposition **в** worked with the prepositional case to indicate the idea of being at the library. The noun in the prepositional case was the object of the preposition.

When **в** comes before the word **библиотéке** the whole thing will sound something like *vbee-blee-a-T ᵛEK-ᵛeh*. The *v* sound goes by quick, so you have to listen carefully! This is a prime example of a time when you really need to listen to the recordings to help you absorb the sounds of the Russian language.

Now let's try a complete sentence.

Светлáна — в библиотéке. *(Svetlana is at the library.)*

In the exercises, watch for the preposition **в**, along with the prepositional case.

EXERCISES

1. **Клáра в библиотéке.**
2. **Екатерúна и Óльга — в библиотéке.**
3. **Он в библиотéке, но онá не в библиотéке.**
4. **Кнúги и газéты в библиотéке.**
5. **Журналúстка — в библиотéке.**
6. **Мне не нрáвятся библиотéки. Мне не нрáвятся кнúги.**
7. **Вы покáзываете библиотéку Натáше.**
8. **Мне нрáвятся кóшки, но Óльге не нрáвятся кóшки.**
9. **Мы покáзываем библиотéку студéнткам. Студéнткам нрáвится библиотéка.**
10. **Э́то кнúги дéвочек.**

Answers on page 265.

LESSON 132

THE PREPOSITIONAL PLURAL

If you want to say that people are in more than one place, you will need to use the prepositional case, but in the plural. The ending of the prepositional plural consists of the letter **а** *(ah)* along with the letter **х** *(cha)*. You haven't seen the letter **х** *(cha)* in a while—it's the letter that has a whooshing sound in the back of the mouth.

Here is what the prepositional plural form of **библиотéка** looks like:

библиотéках

So when you pronounce it, it will sound something like *bee-blee-a-TʸEK-ach* (watch out for the **х** *(cha)* on the last syllable).

	Singular	Plural
Nominative (subject/pred. nom.)	библиотéка	библиотéки
Genitive (possession)	библиотéки	библиотéк
Dative (ind. obj./obj. of prep.)	библиотéке	библиотéкам
Accusative (direct object)	библиотéку	библиотéки
Prepositional (object of prep.)	библиотéке	библиотéках

Here's a situation in which you would use the prepositional plural form of a noun. Let's say that some female students decide to go and do research at the various libraries at their university. In that case, you might say to someone, *The female students are at the libraries.* You could say this kind of thing in Russian with the preposition **в** and a prepositional plural noun, like this:

в библиотéках *(at the libraries)*

And now here's a complete sentence:

> **Студе́нтки — в библиоте́ках.** *(The female students are at the libraries.)*

EXERCISES

1. **Кни́ги — в библиоте́ках.**
2. **Мы чита́ем кни́ги в библиоте́ках.**
3. **Маши́на в библиоте́ке.**
4. **Де́вочкам нра́вятся кни́ги.**
5. **Мне не нра́вится маши́на Екатери́ны, но мне нра́вится маши́на О́льги.**
6. **Ба́бушка Ната́ши даёт мне еду́.**
7. **Соба́ки меня́ ви́дят!**
8. **Я чита́ю газе́ты в библиоте́ке.**
9. **Же́нщины покупа́ют су́мки.**
10. **Соба́кам де́вочки нра́вится еда́.**

Answers on page 266.

LESSON 133

NEW WORD   **шко́ла**

MEANING   *school*

PRONUNCIATION TIP: This word sounds something like *SHKOH-la*.

This word originally comes from the ancient Greek word *schole* which was a place where people gave lectures. Here's a declension chart for this new word:

	SINGULAR	PLURAL
NOMINATIVE (SUBJECT/PRED. NOM.)	шко́ла	шко́лы
GENITIVE (POSSESSION)	шко́лы	шко́л
DATIVE (IND. OBJ./OBJ. OF PREP.)	шко́ле	шко́лам
ACCUSATIVE (DIRECT OBJECT)	шко́лу	шко́лы
PREPOSITIONAL (OBJECT OF PREP.)	шко́ле	шко́лах

So far, the only noun you know that refers to a place is the word **библиоте́ка**. But now that you know the word **шко́ла**, you have another noun that you can use the preposition **в** with, like this:

Су́мка Кла́ры в шко́ле. *(Clara's purse is at the school.)*

Remember that the preposition **в** is pronounced as if it is joined to the next word. The word **шко́ла** begins with an *sh* sound. Before that particular sound, the preposition **в** will sound more like a quick *f* sound. Therefore the phrase **в шко́ле** will sound something like *FSHKO-lʸeh*.

EXERCISES

1. Девочки в школе.
2. Девочки в школах.
3. Ольга — в школе. Ольге не нравится школа.
4. Собака не в школе.
5. Анна в библиотеке, а Светлана в школе.
6. Женщины — в библиотеках.
7. Мы показываем журналисткам школу. Журналисткам нравится школа.
8. Вы даёте ручки и бумагу школам.
9. Собакам нравится машина.
10. Бабушке Анны нравится еда.

Answers on page 266.

LESSON 134

NEW WORD **я рабо́таю**

MEANING *I work*

PRONUNCIATION TIP: Notice that for all six present tense forms of this verb, the stress is on the second syllable. It sounds like *rah-BO-tah-yoo*.

Here's a verb that you can really work with!

	Singular	Plural
First Person	я рабо́таю	мы рабо́таем
Second Person	ты рабо́таешь	вы рабо́таете
Third Person	он/она́ рабо́тает	они́ рабо́тают

You can use this verb to show where someone works, such as at a library or school. Here are a few example sentences:

- **Светла́на рабо́тает в шко́ле.** *(Svetlana works at the/a school.)*
- **Мы рабо́таем в библиоте́ке.** *(We work at the/a library.)*
- **Вы не рабо́таете в шко́ле.** *(Y'all do not work at the/a school.)*

Don't forget—the preposition **в** is pronounced as if it is joined with the next word.

EXERCISES

1. Кла́ра и Светла́на рабо́тают в библиоте́ке.

2. Же́нщина рабо́тает в шко́ле.

3. Вы рабо́таете в библиоте́ках.

4. Ты рабо́таешь в шко́ле, а я рабо́таю в библиоте́ке.

5. Соба́кам нра́вится маши́на.

6. Екатери́на ви́дит меня́, но я не ви́жу Екатери́ну.

7. Мы пока́зываем шко́лу Кла́ры де́вочкам.

8. Ко́шке О́льги не нра́вится еда́.

9. Светла́не не нра́вятся кни́ги. Она́ даёт кни́ги библиоте́ке.

10. Мне нра́вятся соба́ки, а Ната́ше нра́вятся ко́шки.

Answers on page 266.

LESSON 135

NEW WORD   **где**

MEANING   *where*

PRONUNCIATION TIP: This word only has one syllable, but it has several sounds crammed into that one syllable. It has a *g* sound followed immediately by a *d* sound, so it sounds something like *g'd'eh*.

Now that you know how to say *where* in Russian, you can begin to ask your first questions! For example, if you want to ask where the dog is, you could say this:

Где соба́ка? *(Where is the dog?)*

Or, you could ask where Svetlana is, like this:

Где Светла́на? *(Where is Svetlana?)*

You can even ask where someone works, like this:

Где Екатери́на рабо́тает? *(Where does Catherine work?)*

In a question like that one, the word order may vary. For example, you may see a question worded with the verb before the subject, like this:

Где рабо́тает Екатери́на? *(Where does Catherine work?)*

Before we go to the exercises, we would like to make a quick observation about pronunciation. When native English speakers ask a question, the pitch of the speaker's voice will often (not always) rise toward the end of the sentence. For example, if you say *Are you going to visit your Aunt Martha next Tuesday?* then the pitch of your voice will probably rise as you approach the end of the sentence.

But when native Russian speakers ask questions, the rise and fall of the pitch of the voice is not the same as in English. A Russian speaker may emphasize the word being asked about by raising the pitch of the voice on that particular word, and then the pitch of the voice will go down toward the end of the question. So don't be surprised if the rise and fall of the voice in a Russian sentence sounds very different than what you are used to! Be sure to listen carefully to the recordings so you can hear what we are talking about.

EXERCISES

1. Где ко́шка?

2. Где рабо́тает Ната́ша?

3. Где А́нна и О́льга?

4. Где вы рабо́таете?

5. Мы рабо́таем в шко́лах, а А́нна рабо́тает в библиоте́ках.

6. Я в шко́ле, но Кла́ра не в шко́ле.

7. Ба́бушка Ната́ши даёт еду́ Ната́ше.

8. Ко́шка меня́ ви́дит. Мне не нра́вятся ко́шки.

9. Де́вочкам не нра́вится маши́на А́нны.

10. Э́то ко́шка.

Answers on page 266.

LESSON 136

NEW WORD **больни́ца**

MEANING *hospital*

PRONUNCIATION TIP: This word has the stress on the second syllable, so it sounds something like *balʸ-Nʸ EE-tsa*. Note that the **л** *(el)* in this word is soft (palatalized).

Our new word for this lesson is just what the doctor ordered! Now we have yet another place to make sentences about.

	Singular	Plural
Nominative (subject/pred. nom.)	больни́ца	больни́цы
Genitive (possession)	больни́цы	больни́ц
Dative (ind. obj./obj. of prep.)	больни́це	больни́цам
Accusative (direct object)	больни́цу	больни́цы
Prepositional (object of prep.)	больни́це	больни́цах

EXERCISES

1. **Ба́бушка Светла́ны в больни́це.**
2. **О́льга рабо́тает в больни́це.**
3. **Ты не рабо́таешь в больни́це.**
4. **Где ты рабо́таешь? Я рабо́таю в больни́цах.**

5. Где Óльга? Онá не в библиотéке.

6. Екатерúна покупáет собáку.

7. Жéнщины рабóтают в больнúце.

8. Дéвочкам не нрáвится больнúца.

9. Меня́ зовýт Áнна. Я рабóтаю в библиотéке.

10. Натáша и Клáра даю́т кнúги библиотéкам и больнúцам.

Answers on page 267.

LESSON 137

PREPOSITIONS AREN'T JUST FOR THE PREPOSITIONAL CASE

So far you have used the prepositional case with the preposition **в** to say that someone is "at" someplace, such as a school, library, or hospital. And that's marvelous and fabulous…but the fact that the prepositional case has the name "prepositional" is somewhat misleading. With that name, you might think that it's the only case that can be used with prepositions. But, strange as it may seem, the reality is that every noun case except the nominative case can be the object of a preposition. The thing that really makes the prepositional case prepositional is the fact that it cannot stand by itself—it must always be accompanied by a preposition, whereas the other cases don't have to be accompanied by a preposition.

If you continue your study of Russian, you will encounter many more prepositions. When you do, you will have to remember what case each new preposition works with. In the meantime, however, in this book you will only learn one preposition.

LESSON 138

TWO-WAY PREPOSITIONS

In the last lesson, you learned that out of the six Russian noun cases, five of them can be used with prepositions. But wait! There's more!

Certain Russian prepositions can work with more than one noun case—and these prepositions can mean different things depending on which case they take. For example, a preposition might mean one thing if it takes the dative case, but another thing if it takes the accusative case. Prepositions that can take two different cases are called *two-way prepositions*.

As it turns out, the only preposition you know so far is a two-way preposition. When **в** takes the prepositional case, it can mean *at* or *in*. But when it takes the accusative case, it means *to*. Let's look at a few examples to see how this works.

You already know how this one works:

в шко́ле *(at the school)*

In that example, since the preposition **в** was followed by the prepositional case, it meant *at*, and so we translated it as *at the school*.

Now let's see what happens when we use **в** with the accusative case:

в шко́лу *(to the school)*

In that example, since the preposition **в** was followed by the accusative case, it meant *to*, and so we translated the prepositional phrase as *to the school*.

So you see, the different noun cases have different shades of meaning. When used with prepositions, the accusative case is used to show movement toward something, while the prepositional case is used to show where something is located.

The basic idea here is that, to fully understand the meaning of a preposition, sometimes you need to look not only at the preposition itself, but also at the case that the following noun is taking.

LESSON 139

NEW WORD **я иду́**

MEANING *I go, I am going*

PRONUNCIATION TIP: Notice that all the verbs in the chart below have the accent on the verb's personal ending. **иду́** sounds something like *eee-DOO*.

Our new verb for this lesson is similar to the verb **я даю́** *(give)* because four out of the six present tense forms contain the letter **ё** *(yo)*. As we mentioned before, when a syllable contains that letter, that syllable receives the stress, so there is no need to mark that syllable with an accent mark.

	SINGULAR	PLURAL
FIRST PERSON	я иду́	мы идём
SECOND PERSON	ты идёшь	вы идёте
THIRD PERSON	он/она́ идёт	они́ иду́т

In the last lesson, you learned that the preposition **в** can mean different things depending on what case the following noun takes. If **в** takes the prepositional case, it can mean *at*, but if it takes the accusative case, it can mean *to*.

Since you know how to say that someone is going somewhere using the verb **иду́**, let's try to put together some complete sentences in which someone is going somewhere. We will use the preposition **в** along with the accusative case to communicate the idea of going "to" someplace. Here's an example:

Я иду́ в больни́цу. *(I am going to the hospital.)*

In that example, the preposition **в** means *to* because it is working with the accusative case.

One other thing to notice is that this particular verb indicates that someone is going somewhere right now. In lesson 91 we mentioned that present tense verbs in Russian can be translated using the simple present or the present progressive. But for this particular verb, the meaning is really present progressive. In other words, **иду́** should be translated as *I am going*, not with the simple present as *I go*.

In the following exercises you will see the preposition **в** often. Pay special attention to the case that the noun following **в** is taking. Does it take the prepositional case or the accusative case? Does it mean *at* or *to*?

EXERCISES

1. **А́нна в шко́ле.**
2. **А́нна идёт в шко́лу.**
3. **Екатери́на в больни́це.**
4. **Екатери́на идёт в больни́цу.**
5. **Где ба́бушка Кла́ры? Она́ не в больни́це.**
6. **Я иду́ в библиоте́ку.**
7. **Я в библиоте́ке.**
8. **Екатери́на и Светла́на иду́т в больни́цу.**
9. **Кла́ре нра́вятся соба́ки, а Светла́не нра́вятся ко́шки.**
10. **Мы идём в библиоте́ку.**

Answers on page 267.

LESSON 140

EXPRESSING MEANS OR INSTRUMENT

In English, we have different ways of expressing the means or instrument used to accomplish a task. Consider the following examples:

- I hit the nail <u>with a hammer</u>.
- I traveled to the island <u>by boat</u>.
- We fooled the guard <u>by means of trickery</u>.

In each of the above examples, we used *with*, *by*, or *by means of* to express the means or instrument used to accomplish a task.

In the following exercises, a certain phrase is underlined. Some of these underlined phrases are examples of means or instrument, while others are not. Can you identify which exercises contain an example of means or instrument? Be careful—a few of them are tricky! If you find a certain exercise difficult, just ask yourself this question: is someone using the underlined noun as a tool or instrument to accomplish a task, or not? (Try this out with numbers 3 and 4 below!)

EXERCISES

1. We went to Philadelphia <u>by train</u>.
2. We rode the train <u>to Philadelphia.</u>
3. I went to the park <u>with my frisbee</u>.
4. I scared away the squirrel <u>with my frisbee</u>.
5. Julia went to the store <u>with her credit card</u>.
6. Julia picked the lock <u>with her credit card</u>.
7. I convinced them <u>with logic</u>.
8. Harvey poked the chipmunk <u>with a stick</u>.
9. Harvey is standing over there <u>with a stick</u>.
10. Sheila is sitting over there <u>by the boat</u>.

Answers on page 267.

LESSON 141

THE INSTRUMENTAL CASE

In Russian, we express means or instrument with the fifth of the six cases which is called the *instrumental case*.

In English, you might use these words to show that you are using a certain object to accomplish a task:

- with
- by
- by means of

But in Russian, you don't need extra words like that—instead, you can use the instrumental case. The idea of *by means of* is embedded in the instrumental case, so the instrumental case can express that concept by itself, without the help of any extra words such as *with*, *by*, or *by means of*.

In the chart below, observe the instrumental singular form of the noun **ру́чка**, which means *pen*.

	Singular	Plural
Nominative (subject/pred. nom.)	ру́чка	ру́чки
Genitive (possession)	ру́чки	ру́чек
Dative (ind. obj./obj. of prep.)	ру́чке	ру́чкам
Accusative (direct object)	ру́чку	ру́чки
Instrumental (means/obj. of prep.)	**ру́чкой**	
Prepositional (object of prep.)	ру́чке	ру́чках

This instrumental singular ending of **ой** might look familiar, but it has been a while since you have seen it. Back in lesson 33, we gave you a chart that showed how the **й** *(ee kratkoyeh)* combines with vowels to make various sounds. The letter pair **ой** results in the *oy* sound, as in *boy*. Therefore, the word **ру́чкой** sounds like *ROOCH-koy* (but remember that the last syllable is not stressed, so don't emphasize the *oy* sound too much).

Imagine that you want to say this in Russian:

>I am writing with a pen.

For the word *pen*, you would use the word **ру́чка** but you would have to put it in the instrumental case to show that it is the means or instrument being used to accomplish the task.

Right now, you don't know any Russian verbs that you can use the instrumental case with—so in the meantime, here's a sentence that contains English and Russian mixed together just so you can start to get a feeling for how the instrumental case is used in a sentence.

>I am writing **ру́чкой** (I am writing with a pen.)

In that sentence, the word **ру́чкой** was in the instrumental case, so we translated it into English as *with a pen*. We also could have translated it as *by means of a pen*, but that's a bit wordy. The simplest way to translate the instrumental case into English is with the word *with*.

By the way, there are other ways to use the instrumental case in Russian, but we felt that this particular usage was the best way to introduce you to this case. As you become more advanced in your Russian studies, you'll learn other ways to use the instrumental case.

LESSON 142

NEW WORD   **я пишу́**

MEANING   *I write, I am writing*

PRONUNCIATION TIP: Notice that these verbs have their accent on the first syllable except for the first person singular form. **Пишу́** sounds something like *pee-SHOO*.

It's a long story, but this Russian verb is a distant relative of our English word *picture*. That's because this particular verb can not only mean *to write*, but also *to paint*.

After you learn this verb, you'll have all the "write" ingredients for making new sentences.

	Singular	Plural
First Person	я пишу́	мы пи́шем
Second Person	ты пи́шешь	вы пи́шете
Third Person	он/она́ пи́шет	они́ пи́шут

Now that you know how the instrumental case works, you can use our new word for this lesson to make sentences like this:

Кла́ра пи́шет ру́чкой. *(Clara is writing <u>with a pen</u>.)*

Since Clara is using the pen to write with, the word for *pen* is in the instrumental case. Therefore when we translate the sentence into English, we need to put the word *with* in our translation to show that she is writing with the pen.

EXERCISES

1. Ты пи́шешь ру́чкой.

2. Студе́нтка пи́шет ру́чкой.

3. О́льга и Екатери́на пи́шут ру́чкой.

4. Мы пи́шем.

5. Вы пи́шете, а мы чита́ем.

6. Где ру́чка?

7. Кла́ра рабо́тает в больни́це, а А́нна рабо́тает в библиоте́ке.

8. Я не пишу́ ру́чкой. Мне не нра́вятся ру́чки.

9. Де́вочке не нра́вится шко́ла.

10. Студе́нткам не нра́вится кни́га А́нны.

Answers on page 267.

LESSON 143

THE INSTRUMENTAL PLURAL

This is an exciting lesson because we have now filled in the entire noun declension chart! Congratulations to you!

OK, party's over—back to work! The instrumental plural has the ending **-ами** which sounds like *ah-me*. You can use the instrumental plural if more than one object is being used.

	Singular	Plural
Nominative (subject/pred. nom.)	ру́чка	ру́чки
Genitive (possession)	ру́чки	ру́чек
Dative (ind. obj./obj. of prep.)	ру́чке	ру́чкам
Accusative (direct object)	ру́чку	ру́чки
Instrumental (means/obj. of prep.)	ру́чкой	*ру́чками*
Prepositional (object of prep.)	ру́чке	ру́чках

Here's an example of the instrumental plural being used in a sentence.

Же́нщины пи́шут ру́чками. *(The women are writing with (the) pens.)*

EXERCISES

1. **Де́вочки пи́шут ру́чками.**

2. **Студе́нтки пи́шут ру́чками.**

3. **Кла́ра не пи́шет ру́чкой. Кла́ре не нра́вятся ру́чки.**

4. Мы пи́шем ру́чками.

5. А́нна и Ната́ша рабо́тают в больни́це.

6. Де́вочки иду́т в шко́лу.

7. Де́вочки в шко́ле. Де́вочкам не нра́вится шко́ла.

8. Где рабо́тает Екатери́на?

9. Екатери́на и Ната́ша рабо́тают в библиоте́ке.

10. Же́нщины мне пока́зывают су́мки, но мне не нра́вятся су́мки.

Answers on page 268.

LESSON 144

REVIEW OF CASES

You have reached an important milestone—you now know all six noun cases in the Russian language. Let's take a moment to review each of the six cases.

NOMINATIVE

The first case listed in a noun declension chart is the nominative case. The nominative case is used when a noun is the subject or predicate nominative in a sentence. This is how a noun looks when you look it up in a dictionary or on the internet. It is the only case that does not work with prepositions. In the example sentence below, the name *Anna* is in the nominative case because Anna is the subject of the sentence.

Áнна в библиотéке. (*Anna is at the/a library.*)

GENITIVE

The second case listed in a noun declension chart is the genitive case. This case shows possession—that something belongs to someone or something. A genitive noun usually comes right after the noun it possesses. When you translate it into English, you will need to use either an apostrophe and the letter *s* (as seen in the word *Fred's*) or the word *of* (as seen in the phrase *of the mountain*). In the example below, the name *Clara* is in the genitive case because Clara is possessing the pen.

рýчка Клáры (*Clara's pen*)

The genitive case can also be used with certain prepositions.

DATIVE

The third case listed in a noun declension chart is the dative case. The dative case is used in Russian to indicate the indirect object in a sentence. The indirect object is the party in the sentence that is receiving or benefiting. In the example below, the name *Svetlana* is in the dative case because Svetlana is receiving the pen.

Я даю́ ру́чку Светла́не. *(I am giving the/a pen to Svetlana.)*

The dative case can also be used with certain prepositions.

ACCUSATIVE

The fourth case listed in a noun declension chart is the accusative case. The accusative case is used to indicate the direct object. In the example below, the car is in the accusative case because it is the direct object.

Я ви́жу маши́ну. *(I see the/a car.)*

The accusative case can also be used with certain prepositions.

INSTRUMENTAL

The fifth case listed in a noun declension chart is the instrumental case. The instrumental case indicates that a certain object is being used as a tool or instrument. In the example below, the pen is in the instrumental case in order to express that it is being used to perform a task.

Я пишу́ ру́чкой. *(I write with the/a pen.)*

The instrumental case can also be used with certain prepositions.

PREPOSITIONAL

The sixth case listed in a noun declension chart is the prepositional case. The name of this case is something of a misnomer because it is not the only case that can work with prepositions. When the preposition **в** is used with the prepositional case, it means *at*, as seen in this sentence:

Кла́ра — в библиоте́ке. *(Clara is at the/a library.)*

The prepositional case cannot stand by itself—it must be accompanied by a preposition.

LESSON 145

HOW TO SAY "I HAVE" SOMETHING

In English, if you want to say that you have something, you would structure your sentence like this:

>I have a car.

In that sentence the word *I* is the subject, the word *have* is the verb, and *car* is the direct object. But in Russian, this kind of sentence would have a different structure. Here is a word-for-word translation of how that kind of sentence would be worded in Russian.

>By me there is a car.

So, in order to say this kind of thing in Russian, you'll have to learn a thing or two. First, you'll need to learn the word that means *by*. Here it is:

>**у**

This word, like several of the other words you have learned in this book, is also a letter of the alphabet. You know this letter as the letter **у** *(ooh)*.

The preposition **у** takes the genitive case, so if we want to say *by me* in Russian, we need to know the genitive form of the pronoun that means *I* or *me* in Russian. In lesson 123 we talked about how pronouns can be in different cases just like nouns. Also, you learned the dative pronoun **мне** and the accusative pronoun **меня́**. But now, in addition to dative and accusative, we need the genitive form, too. Observe the genitive form of this pronoun in the chart below.

Nominative (subject/pred. nom.)	я
Genitive (possession)	(меня́)
Dative (ind. obj./obj. of prep.)	мне
Accusative (direct object)	меня́

As you can see, the genitive form **меня́** is the same as the accusative form, which is also **меня́**.

Now we are ready to put the preposition **у** and the genitive pronoun **меня́** together into a prepositional phrase:

у меня́

This phrase means *by me* and sounds something like *ooh-mee-NᵞAH*.

The next ingredient we need is the Russian word that means *there is*. Here it is:

есть

This word sounds something like *yest*. Notice that the last character in this word is the soft sign, so the **т** *(te)* will be pronounced with the tongue raised for a more palatalized sound.

Let's put together what we have so far:

У меня́ есть... *(By me there is...)*

This phrase so far sounds something like *oooh-mee-NᵞAH YEST*.

Only one thing is missing now, and that is the thing that is being possessed. Notice that in English, if you say *I have...*, then the thing you have is the direct object in the sentence. But in Russian the sentence structure is different, and we are literally saying *By me there is...*. Therefore in Russian, the thing being possessed is really the subject of the sentence, so it needs to be in the nominative case. So let's add the Russian word for *car* (in the nominative case) to our sentence.

У меня́ есть маши́на. *(By me there is a car.)*

Again, a word-for-word translation of this phrase would be *By me there is a car*, but when we translate it into English, we put the words into a natural-sounding order: *I have a car*.

Now that you understand the basic structure of this kind of sentence, you should practice it a few times to get the feel of it. Think of it as a stock phrase in which only the last word changes, depending on what it is that you have. In the boxes below, we have provided some sample sentences that show the Russian phrase, a word-for-word translation for reference, and then its normal English translation. Try to repeat these phrases over and over until you can say them from memory. Then, try to change the last word in the phrase to some other word—now you're learning to make your own Russian sentences!

EXERCISES

1. У меня́ есть соба́ка.
2. У меня́ есть су́мка.
3. У меня́ есть ко́шка. Мне нра́вятся ко́шки.
4. У меня́ есть маши́на.
5. Ната́ше нра́вится маши́на, но А́нне не нра́вится маши́на.
6. Мы пи́шем ру́чками.
7. Ко́шка в библиоте́ке.
8. Где журнали́стки?
9. Вы не ви́дете ба́бушку Кла́ры.
10. Актри́са покупа́ет маши́ну.

Answers on page 268.

LESSON 146

I DON'T HAVE IT!

Imagine that you want to say this:

> I do not have a car.

Here is a word-for-word translation of how this kind of sentence will read in Russian:

> By me there is not (any) of car.

It's sort of like in English when we say something like *I don't have any of your money* or *I don't have any of the books*.

In Russian, this kind of sentence will start out the same as before, when you learned how to say that you have something:

> **у меня́** *(by me)*

But the next word is different—instead of having a verb that says *there is*, we need to have a negative verb that says *there is not*. Here is the word that means *there is not*:

> **нет** *(there is not)*

This word sounds like *nʸet*, and means *there is not*. (By the way, if this word looks familiar, it is also the word for *no* in Russian, which we mentioned briefly in lesson 29).

So what we have so far would add up to this:

> **У меня́ нет...** *(By me there is not...)*

This phrase so far sounds something like *oooh-mee-NʸAH NʸET*.

This last ingredient is kind of unusual, so pay attention: the thing that you are saying that you don't have must be in the genitive case. This is because the idea is

234

that you don't have "any of" something. The idea of *of* is supplied by the genitive case.

У меня́ нет маши́ны. *(By me there is not (any) of car.)*

Again, this is a word-for-word translation of the Russian. If you were actually translating this sentence into English, you would translate it as *I do not have the car* or *I do not have a car*.

The main thing we would like you to remember here is that when you say you have something, the thing being possessed is in the nominative case. But if you say you don't have something, the thing being (not) possessed is in the genitive case.

You'll need some practice with this new kind of statement, so here are some sample sentences you can repeat over and over for practice.

By me there is not (any) of book.

I do not have the/a book.

By me there is not (any) of purse.

I do not have the/a purse.

By me there is not (any) of cat.

I do not have the/a cat.

By me there is not (any) of pen.

I do not have the/a pen.

EXERCISES

1. У меня́ нет ко́шки. У меня́ есть соба́ка.

2. У соба́ки нет еды́.

3. У ко́шки есть еда́ соба́ки!

4. А́нна идёт в шко́лу. Кла́ра в шко́ле.

5. У меня́ нет су́мки. Же́нщина пока́зывает мне су́мку.

6. У ба́бушки Ната́ши есть соба́ка.

7. Соба́ки не ви́дят меня́.

8. Где рабо́тают спортсме́нки?

9. Меня́ зову́т О́льга. Э́то Екатери́на.

10. Мы не в библиоте́ке.

Answers on page 268.

LESSON 147

FORMAL AND INFORMAL SPEECH

This book is almost finished—but before we go, there is one last important thing we need to teach you: the difference between informal and formal speech in Russian.

In every society, there are different levels of social formality. For example, when you talk to your friends and family, you might use all kinds of slang and other colloquial words and phrases such as *Dude!* and *What's up?* But what if you had the chance to meet a king, queen, or president of a country? Would you speak to that person in the same familiar, informal way that you would speak to your friends? Probably not! Instead, you would probably address a president with courteous, respectful speech, perhaps saying words such as *sir* or *ma'am*.

Practically speaking, it all boils down to social closeness or social familiarity. In other words, there is a way to speak Russian to people who are socially close to you, and a way to speak Russian to people who are more socially distant from you. This is an important thing for any student of the Russian language to understand—that's because whenever you speak Russian with someone, you must be socially aware of whether that conversation should be considered formal or informal. Why is this? Because the way you view the relationship between you and the person you are talking to will be reflected in your choice of words. If you are speaking to someone whom you view as socially close, you will use certain pronouns and verb forms that reflect that close relationship. But if you are speaking to someone whom you view as socially distant, you will use certain other pronouns and verb forms that reflect that feeling of distance. In this way, the use of the language itself reflects whether the relationship is close and informal or more distant and formal.

Russian is not the only language that has these differing levels of formality reflected by pronoun and verb usage. French, Spanish, and German all have similar manners of speech associated with social closeness or distance. Those of you who have studied French before will be at an advantage here because the way formal speech is done in Russian is the same, grammatically speaking, as the way it is done in French.

When should you use formal speech in Russian? Here are some of the situations in which formal speech is expected:

- When speaking with someone you don't know very well
- When speaking with someone older than you
- When speaking with your boss at work
- When speaking with a professor or teacher
- When speaking with someone in a position of authority

When in doubt, use formal speech. The use of informal speech can unintentionally come across as rude if used in an inappropriate setting. Native Russian speakers will be happy to let you know when it is okay to switch to informal speech, so follow their lead!

LESSON 148

THE MECHANICS OF FORMAL SPEECH

In the last lesson, we introduced the concept of social closeness or familiarity in Russian, and how this can affect speech. But how do you use and apply formal speech in Russian? What are the specific grammatical differences between speaking informally in Russian and speaking formally?

Here is the key to speaking formally in Russian: instead of using second person singular pronouns and verbs, you must use second person *plural* pronouns and verbs. In English, it would be like addressing someone as *y'all* instead of *you*, treating them as plural instead of singular. Somehow, addressing someone in a plural way establishes a feeling of social distance. If you address someone using the second person singular, it feels close and personal. But if you address someone using the second person plural, it feels more distant and formal.

All the exercises in this book so far have used informal speech. We did this for a reason—we wanted you to understand the literal, concrete meanings of pronouns and verbs before teaching you to use them in other ways that are more abstract. But now that you are learning how formal speech works in Russian, you need to begin to learn how to associate the different Russian pronouns and verbs with formal and informal speech.

Here's an example: if you were speaking to a friend, a family member, or a child, and you wanted to say the word *you*, you would use the second person singular pronoun **ты**. But if you were speaking to someone in a position of authority, someone older than you, or someone you didn't know very well, you would use the second person plural pronoun **вы**.

Let's do a little exercise to help you observe how these grammatical differences would work in everyday conversations. Let's pretend that your sister just got a new job, and you would like to know where she works. You want to say *Where do you work?* Since your sister is someone socially close to you, you can address her with informal speech, using the second person singular pronoun **ты** plus a second person singular verb, like this:

Где ты работаешь? *(Where do you work?)*

That would be considered informal speech because it was all in the second person singular.

Now let's pretend that you are at a party and you meet a gentleman whom you don't know very well and who is much older than you. You want to ask him where he works. In this social situation you should definitely use formal speech. Therefore you should use the second person plural pronoun **вы** plus a second person plural verb.

Где вы работаете? *(Where do you work?)*

Even though you are speaking to only one person, using a second person plural pronoun and verb communicates a feeling of social distance that is appropriate for this conversation.

Of course, if you were addressing more than one person, you would need to use the pronoun **вы** whether it's a formal or informal situation.

LESSON 149

FORMAL GREETINGS AND PHRASES

So far, the greetings and phrases that we have taught you are all considered to be informal. Words such as **пока́** *(bye!)*, **приве́т** *(hi / hello)*, and **здра́вствуй** *(hello)* are all expressions that can fit into a conversation with people that you are socially close to.

But now that you know how formal speech works in Russian, we can show you some additional greetings that are more formal, and therefore more appropriate for conversations in which you are meeting new people or speaking to those whom you don't know very well.

Here's a formal way to say *good day*:

до́брый день

In the first word of that expression, the letter combination **ый** sounds much like the regular **ы** *(y)*, except that you may hear a slight palatalization at the end of the word since the **й** is present. In the second word, notice that there is a soft sign at the end, so the **н** *(en)* will be palatalized. Therefore, the expression sounds something like *DOH-br(y) d^yen^y*. It's a simple expression—the word **до́брый** means *good* and the word **день** means *day*, so literally it means *good day*. It's no coincidence that the word **день** starts with a *d* sound like our English word *day*, because the two words are distant relatives.

Here is a formal way to say *good morning*:

до́брое у́тро

The first word ends with two vowels that you have not seen put together yet: **ое**. These letters do not combine into one sound. Instead, they are pronounced separately as an unstressed **о** *(oh)* (which will sound like *ah*) followed by the **е** *(yeh)*. At the end of the second word, the **о** *(oh)* at the end is after the stress, so it will sound like an *uh*. Put all of that together, and this expression sounds something like *DOH-bra-yeh OOOH-truh*. The word **до́брое** means *good*, and **у́тро** means *morning*. You may have noticed that in this expression, the word for *good* is spelled differently than in the expression **до́брый день**. That's because the word for *morning* (**у́тро**) is neuter while the word for *day* (**день**) is masculine. In Russian, endings of adjectives change depending on gender, case, and number, just as nouns do, and the adjective must be in the same grammatical gender as the noun it describes.

Here's a formal way to say *good evening*:

до́брый ве́чер

This expression sounds something like *DOH-br(y)-VʸEH-cher*. Just as we saw before, the word **до́брый** means *good* while the word **ве́чер** means *evening*, so literally it means *good evening*. The word **ве́чер** is a distant relative of our English word *vesper* which refers to the evening or something that happens in the evening. The noun **ве́чер** is masculine just like **день**, so the word for *good* here is the same form as in the expression **до́брый день**.

There's one other thing we would like to mention—a new word that you can use as a formal way to say hello to someone.

здра́вствуйте

This word can be difficult to pronounce because it has several different consonant sounds crammed together. The first syllable sounds something like *zdravst*. Yes, that's six consonants packed into one syllable—but if it makes you feel any better, it's really just two three-consonant clusters, not six unrelated consonants.

Now you may be saying to yourself, *Hey! Wait a minute! That's an informal greeting that you taught me way back in lesson 87!* Well, that's partially true. You see, this greeting has two forms, one singular and one plural. Just as we saw with pronouns, the singular one is for informal situations, while the plural one is for formal situations or for any time you are greeting more than one person (whether formal or not). Look carefully at the two different forms of this greeting, paying special attention to the ending of the word.

- **здра́вствуй** (informal)
- **здра́вствуйте** (formal)

The difference is because of the distinction between informal and formal speech in Russian. This greeting is based on a verb which means *be well* or *prosper*. The form of the verb is an imperative—in other words, it's a command. When you say it to someone, you are telling them *Be well!*

And finally, here's a formal way to say *goodbye*.

до свида́ния

This expression sounds something like *da sve-DAHN-yah*. It literally means *Until the next meeting*.

LESSON 150

WHAT'S YOUR NAME?

In the last lesson, we looked at a few formal greetings, and we even saw one greeting in particular that has both an informal version and a formal version. The last phrase we would like to teach you in this book is how to ask what someone's name is. This phrase falls into the category of formal speech because, if you think about it, the question itself implies that you don't know the person very well. After all, if you already know someone well, you probably know the person's name! So, for that reason, we wanted to teach you this expression in the part of the book that deals with formal speech.

In English, if you wanted to ask what someone's name is, you would structure the sentence like this:

> What is your name?

This sentence has the verb *is*, which is a verb of being. In Russian, however, this kind of sentence is worded differently. Here is a word-for-word translation of how you would structure this question in Russian:

> How you they call?

This sentence structure is different, grammatically speaking. Here, the verb is not a verb of being, but the action verb *call*. Also notice that the word *you* is the direct object in this sentence.

Let's start putting this sentence together in Russian. First, we need the Russian word for *how*, which is **как**. So our Russian sentence would start out like this:

Как...? *(How...?)*

Now we need the Russian word for *you*. Of course you already know the pronoun **вы**, but that particular word won't work here. The pronoun **вы** is nominative, but here we need the accusative form because the word *you* in this sentence is a direct object. So what we really need here is the word **вас**, which is the accusative form of **вы**. The word **вас** sounds like *vahss*. Let's plug it into our Russian sentence:

Как вас...? (How you...?)

Finally, we need to know how to say *they call* in Russian. But you already know this particular word—you learned it back in lesson 89 when you learned how to say sentences like *My name is Anna*. It's the third person plural verb **зову́т** (pronounced *za-VOOT*) and it means *they call* in Russian. Let's add **зову́т** to our sentence:

Как вас зову́т? (How you they call?)

The sentence is now complete! Again, literally it would say *How you they call?* But it is the equivalent of saying *What is your name?* in English.

The phrase **Как вас зову́т?** is formal speech, but there is also an informal way to say it. Say, for example, that an adult wants to say "What's your name?" to a child. In that situation, the adult would probably use informal speech. Here's how this phrase would look but with informal speech instead of formal speech:

Как тебя́ зову́т? (How you they call?)

In the formal version of this phrase, we have the pronoun **вас**, which is plural. As we mentioned before, **вас** is the accusative form of the plural pronoun **вы**. But the informal version of this phrase uses the pronoun **тебя́**, which is singular. The word **тебя́** is the accusative form of the singular pronoun **ты**.

In this lesson, we could have just given you the entire Russian sentence all at once, and then said *Memorize this phrase!* But in this book, we don't just want you to memorize and regurgitate phrases that you don't understand. When we teach you something, we want you to fully understand each ingredient in the phrase so that you understand the structure of that phrase. Also, this allows you to build more connections with the other phrases that you know, and the ones you will learn in the future.

LESSON 151

FORMAL NAMES IN RUSSIAN

As long as we are on the subject of formal speech in Russian, we ought to tell you a little about how names work in Russian. But first we need to teach you a new word: the word *patronymic*. This word comes to us from Greek roots. The *patr-* part of the word is from the ancient Greek word that means *father*. That particular root word can be found in other words such as *patriarchy* and *patrilineal*. The *-onym-* part of the word is from the ancient Greek word that means *name*. That root word can be found in other words such as *homonym* and *synonym*. Therefore the word *patronymic* literally means *father-name*. It generally means a name that is derived from the first name of someone's father. Keep that in mind as we go along.

The reason that you need to know the word *patronymic* is that it is a big part of the way you address someone formally in Russian. In English, we address people by their personal name (first name) and then their last name (also known as a family name or surname). For someone named Fred Smith, his personal name is Fred and Smith is a family name—a name that everyone in his family shares. In a situation where Fred Smith is in a position of authority, we refer to him as *Mr. Smith*. But in a formal Russian conversation, when you address someone, you address them by their first name and then their patronymic.

Let's say that you meet someone named Olga. Olga's family name is Pavlova. But you would not address her as Olga Pavlova. Instead, you would address her as Olga and then her patronymic—that is, a name that is formed from her father's first name. So if her father's first name is Ivan, you would call her Olga Ivanovna. The *-ovna* ending means *daughter of*. Now let's say that Olga has a brother named Boris. He would be formally addressed as Boris Ivanovich. As you may have guessed, the *-ovich* ending means *son of*. Addressing these two people as Olga Ivanovna and Boris Ivanovich shows respect, in much the same way as when English speakers refer to someone as Ms. Smith or Mr. Smith.

Interestingly, Russian is not the only language in which patronymics are used. In fact, in Iceland, people don't even have family names or surnames—instead, they have a first name and then a patronymic. The patronymic is just the father's first name, the letter *s* to show possession, and then either the suffix *-son* or *-dóttir* added to the end. So an Icelandic woman named Helga whose father's first name is Gunnar would be named Helga Gunnarsdóttir. An Icelandic man named Jóhann whose father's first name is Einar would be Jóhann Einarsson.

Similar naming systems were formerly used in other Scandanavian countries as well.

So, if you have ever read a Russian novel and wondered what was going on with all the names ending in *-ovna* and *-ovich*, now you know!

GENERAL ADVICE

Congratulations! You made it all the way to the end of the book!

In closing, the authors would like to offer a few thoughts which you may find helpful. This book was designed to cover the beginning stages of Russian grammar in the easiest way possible. However, there is still a lot you do not know. So here are a few thoughts and suggestions to help you continue your study of Russian.

One of the most important ways to grasp the Russian language is to have a strong understanding of how the cases are used. Once you understand the idea that direct objects are in the accusative case, indirect objects are in the dative case, etc., you can apply that same knowledge to the other two declensions. If you go on to learn the second and, later, the third declension, your vocabulary options will grow and you will have more things to talk about in Russian. The way the cases are used will always be the same, but you will have to learn new noun endings for each new declension.

One way to improve your recognition and understanding of the cases and endings is to memorize short sentences that demonstrate a certain grammatical concept. For example, if you memorize **я читáю кни́гу**, you will remember that for first declension nouns, the direct object has the **у** *(ooh)* ending. With that pattern in mind, using the accusative ending for direct objects will become more and more automatic for you.

In order to reduce the need for rote memorization, we have only used a small number of words in this book. Therefore, you should strive to increase your Russian vocabulary. One way to do that is to use Russian in real-life situations. It may be difficult for you to find opportunities to speak Russian, but fortunately, the internet has made it easier to get in contact with other people who share your interests. Check out our website for some links to help you get started.

Lastly, we would like to encourage you to always be aware of your pronunciation so that you can cultivate the most authentic Russian pronunciation possible. One way to do this is to take advantage of the many videos on YouTube which explain and demonstrate Russian pronunciation. Look for links to some of our favorites on our website.

Please take a moment to reflect on all you have learned. You have come a long way from lesson 1, and you are now ready to go further in your Russian studies. We, the authors, sincerely hope that this book has been enjoyable and profitable for you. We also hope that the knowledge you have gained from this book will become the foundation of a lifetime of enjoyment of the Russian language.

ANSWER KEY

LESSON SEVEN

1. mop
2. pot
3. cop
4. papa
5. pop
6. mom
7. Tom
8. mama

LESSON EIGHT

1. me
2. key
3. team/teem
4. meet/meat
5. keep
6. teapot
7. cop
8. pot
9. mop
10. pop

LESSON NINE

1. Bob
2. be/bee
3. beet/beat
4. beak
5. beep
6. me
7. team
8. teapot
9. key
10. peek/peak
11. meet/meat
12. Tom

LESSON TEN

1. seat
2. steep
3. seek
4. steam
5. spots
6. peace/piece
7. beast
8. seem/seam
9. beet/beat
10. mops
11. keep
12. Bob
13. cop
14. meets/meats
15. beak
16. Bobby

LESSON ELEVEN

1. soup
2. moose
3. boom
4. team/teem
5. box
6. Bob
7. ski
8. meets/meats
9. cop
10. beeps
11. stops
12. steep
13. peace/piece
14. seek
15. beet/beat
16. seat

LESSON TWELVE

1. meets/meats
2. beats/beets
3. spots
4. teapots
5. boots
6. mops
7. keeps
8. Bobby
9. me
10. beak
11. team/teem
12. seek
13. stop
14. ski
15. socks
16. boom

LESSON 13

1. leap
2. leak
3. lost
4. sleep
5. eel
6. school
7. pots
8. boots
9. pool
10. Bob
11. meets/meats
12. peace/piece
13. soup
14. spots
15. beeps
16. mops

LESSON 14

1. leaf
2. fool
3. beef
4. flutes
5. floss
6. pots
7. school
8. feast
9. moose
10. beast
11. boots
12. seal
13. eel
14. peel/peal
15. leaps
16. beak
17. seats
18. cops
19. teapots
20. soup

LESSON 15

1. food
2. deal
3. feed
4. seafood
5. deed
6. fool
7. beef
8. feet
9. lots
10. Bobby
11. feats
12. pots
13. feast
14. seats
15. boots
16. feel
17. soup
18. meek
19. meets/meats
20. peel/peal

LESSON 16

1. fed
2. pest
3. led
4. pets
5. bets
6. fell
7. left
8. spell
9. belt
10. deep
11. steal/steel
12. lets/let's
13. seed
14. sets
15. feed
16. boots
17. Bob
18. deal
19. dots
20. cool

LESSON 17

1. moon
2. nets
3. need
4. neck
5. deck
6. bean
7. nest
8. spoon
9. meets/meats
10. steal/steel
11. boots
12. feast
13. pots
14. seed
15. led
16. seafood
17. pool
18. feel
19. seats
20. fed

LESSON 18

1. fuel
2. mule
3. yule
4. feud
5. mute
6. beauty
7. Utah
8. unique
9. few
10. menu
11. nets
12. lets/let's
13. fed
14. said
15. bets
16. dots
17. seal
18. beets/beats
19. bell
20. deed
21. pots
22. seafood
23. need
24. seats

LESSON 23

1. shed
2. chef
3. shock
4. seafood
5. Utah
6. beauty
7. menu
8. mute
9. unique
10. you
11. few
12. east
13. nest
14. beast
15. sets
16. flutes
17. seats
18. dune
19. best
20. pool

LESSON 24

1. cheek
2. cheats
3. beach
4. peach
5. leech
6. chest
7. chief
8. check
9. chef
10. shoots/chutes
11. shed
12. yule
13. lean
14. feud
15. sell/cell
16. desk
17. fell
18. shop
19. food
20. feats

LESSON 26

1. yacht
2. Maya
3. yon
4. papaya
5. cheat
6. chess
7. beach
8. cheek
9. cheap
10. mule
11. seen/scene
12. beauty
13. need
14. shell
15. nest
16. mute
17. pool
18. left
19. sheen
20. food

LESSON 27

1. vet
2. bet
3. leave
4. believe
5. move
6. yon
7. yachts
8. Maya
9. vets
10. chief
11. TV
12. chest
13. fetch
14. feud
15. check
16. fuel
17. shop
18. beauty
19. need
20. keen

LESSON 28

1. goose
2. geese
3. log
4. peg
5. egg nog
6. feud
7. vest
8. cheap
9. believe
10. shots
11. move
12. papaya
13. beach
14. yachts
15. check
16. peach
17. Utah
18. Maya
19. leech
20. Steve

LESSON 29
1. yet
2. yell
3. yes
4. yeti
5. yelp
6. league
7. goose
8. leg
9. chef
10. beg
11. vest
12. leave
13. move
14. vet
15. yon
16. Maya
17. cheap
18. unique
19. beach
20. chief

LESSON 31
1. zoo
2. cheese
3. zoom
4. eggs
5. bees
6. legs
7. yelp
8. yes
9. goose
10. yeti
11. league
12. beg
13. guess
14. papaya
15. believe
16. chest
17. beach
18. yachts
19. leave
20. peach

LESSON 33
1. fight
2. yo-yo
3. Amy
4. boy
5. toy
6. point
7. believe
8. bite
9. easy
10. oil
11. foil
12. papaya
13. move
14. peg
15. Steve
16. best
17. please
18. yelp
19. geese
20. chest

LESSON 34
1. beige
2. massage
3. Jacques
4. espionage
5. luge
6. yo-yo
7. point
8. eggs
9. zoo
10. bite
11. believe
12. Amy
13. yet
14. guess
15. boy
16. log
17. chef
18. toy
19. egg nog
20. papaya
21. yachts
22. chess
23. shock
24. mute

LESSON 43

1. Kate (subject) walks (verb)
2. car (subject) is (verb)
3. sister (subject) likes (verb)
4. horse (subject) is (verb)
5. Harry (subject) told (verb)
6. Bob (subject) plays (verb)
7. Mark (subject) plays (verb)
8. brother (subject) cleans (verb)
9. Julia (subject) loves (verb)
10. students (subject) finished (verb)

LESSON 46

1. ❶ The (the definite article). ❷ The speaker probably has a certain book in mind—asking "Where is a book" probably would not make much sense.
2. ❶ No article. ❷ The speaker is referring to rice in a general sense, not to any specific rice.
3. ❶ A (the indefinite article). ❷ The speaker is probably not referring to a specific pencil—the speaker just wants to have some/any pencil while at school.
4. ❶ The (the definite article). ❷ The lawn being referred to is probably Pat's lawn, not anyone else's lawn.
5. ❶ No article. ❷ Canada is a proper name and so does not require any article to introduce it. There is only one Canada, so there is no need to say "the Canada" or "a Canada."
6. ❶ A (the indefinite article). ❷ The speaker probably does not have any specific cheeseburger in mind—any cheeseburger will do.
7. ❶ A (the indefinite article). ❷ The speaker is speaking about a recurring situation, and the doughnut is not any specific doughnut.
8. ❶ No article. ❷ Saying "I'm late for the school" or "I'm late for a school" just doesn't sound right.
9. ❶ The (the definite article). ❷ The speaker is referring to a certain roof, that is, the speaker's own roof.
10. ❶ A (the indefinite article). ❷ Although the speaker has a certain superhero in mind, the listener apparently doesn't know very much about the movie—therefore the speaker is speaking in general terms.

LESSON 48

1. I
2. I am the/a pilot.
3. I am the/a pilot.

LESSON 49

1. I
2. I am the/a (male) student.
3. I am the/a (male) student.
4. I am the/a pilot.
5. I am the/a pilot.

LESSON 50

1. I
2. I am the/an engineer.
3. I am the/an engineer.
4. I am the/a (male) student.
5. I am the/a (male) student.
6. I am the/a pilot.
7. I am the/a pilot.

LESSON 52

1. I
2. I am the/a journalist.
3. I am the/a journalist.
4. I am the/an engineer.
5. I am the/an engineer.
6. I am the/a (male) student.
7. I am the/a (male) student.
8. I am the/a pilot.
9. I am the/a pilot.

LESSON 53

1. I am the/a pilot.
2. I am not the/a pilot.
3. I am not the/a pilot.
4. I am the/a (male) student.
5. I am not the/a (male) student.
6. I am the/an engineer.
7. I am not the/an engineer.
8. I am the/a journalist.
9. I am not the/a journalist.
10. I am not the/a journalist.

LESSON 54

1. I am the/a diplomat.
2. I am not the/a diplomat.
3. I am not the/a journalist.
4. I am not the/a journalist.
5. I am the/a journalist.
6. I am the/an engineer.
7. I am not the/an engineer.
8. I am the/a (male) student.
9. I am not the/a (male) student.
10. I am the/a pilot.

LESSON 55

1. I am the/a businessperson.
2. I am not the/a businessperson.
3. I am the/a businessperson.
4. I am the/a diplomat.
5. I am not the/a diplomat.
6. I am the/a journalist.
7. I am not the/a journalist.
8. I am not the/an engineer.
9. I am the/a (male) student.
10. I am not the/a pilot.

LESSON 56

1. I am the/a businessperson and the/a diplomat.
2. I am not the/a businessperson.
3. I am the/a diplomat and the/a pilot.
4. I am not the/a diplomat.
5. I am the/a (male) student and the/an engineer.
6. I am not the/an engineer.
7. I am the/a pilot and the/a businessperson.
8. I am not the/a pilot.
9. I am the/a diplomat and the/a businessperson.
10. I am not the/a businessperson.

LESSON 57

1. You
2. You are the/a pilot.
3. You are not the/a journalist.
4. You are not the/a diplomat.
5. You are the/a (male) student and the/an engineer.
6. You are not the/a (male) student.
7. I am the/an engineer and the/a pilot.
8. I am the/a businessperson and the/a (male) student.
9. I am not the/a (male) student.
10. I am the/a diplomat.

LESSON 58

1. He
2. He is not the/a journalist.
3. He is the/a pilot and the/an engineer.
4. He is the/a diplomat.
5. You are the/a businessperson and the/an engineer.
6. You are not the/a businessperson.
7. You are the/an engineer and the/a pilot.
8. You are a pilot and the/a (male) student.
9. I am the/an engineer.
10. I am not the/a (male) student.

LESSON 59

1. She
2. She is the/a pilot and the/a engineer.
3. She is not the/a pilot.
4. He is the/a journalist.
5. He is the/a diplomat and the/a businessperson.
6. He is not the/an engineer.
7. You are not the/a journalist.
8. You are the/a pilot and the/a (male) student.
9. You are not the/a businessperson.
10. I am the/an engineer.

LESSON 60

1. plural
2. singular
3. singular
4. singular
5. plural
6. singular
7. plural
8. plural
9. plural
10. singular

LESSON 61

1. *(the) pilots*
2. *(the) (male) students*
3. *(the) engineers*
4. *(the) journalists*
5. *(the) diplomats*
6. *(the) businesspersons*

LESSON 62

1. *we*
2. *We are not (the) diplomats.*
3. *We are (the) engineers and (the) students.*
4. *We are not (the) businesspersons.*
5. *We are (the) journalists.*
6. *She is not the/a pilot.*
7. *She is the/an engineer and the/a pilot.*
8. *He is a the/a (male) student and the/a journalist.*
9. *You are the/a pilot and the/a (male) student.*
10. *I am the/an engineer.*

LESSON 63

1. *y'all*
2. *Y'all are not (the) diplomats.*
3. *Y'all are (the) pilots.*
4. *We are (the) engineers.*
5. *We are (the) diplomats and (the) businesspersons.*
6. *She is the/an engineer and the/a pilot.*
7. *She is the/an engineer.*
8. *He is the/a pilot and the/a (male) student.*
9. *You are not the/a diplomat.*
10. *I am not the/a businessperson.*

LESSON 64

1. *they*
2. *They are not (the) pilots.*
3. *They are (the) diplomats and (the) businesspersons.*
4. *Y'all are (the) (male) students.*
5. *Y'all are not (the) businesspersons.*
6. *We are (the) engineers and (the) (male) students.*
7. *She is the/a engineer and the/a pilot.*
8. *He is not the/a diplomat.*
9. *You are the/a pilot and the/a (male) student.*
10. *I am the/a businessperson and the/a (male) student.*

LESSON 65

1. ❶ I ❷ first person ❸ singular
2. ❶ you ❷ second person ❸ singular
3. ❶ she ❷ third person ❸ singular
4. ❶ we ❷ first person ❸ plural
5. ❶ y'all ❷ second person ❸ plural
6. ❶ they ❷ third person ❸ plural
7. ❶ he ❷ third person ❸ singular
8. ❶ it ❷ third person ❸ singular
9. ❶ y'all ❷ second person ❸ plural
10. ❶ flowers ❷ third person ❸ plural

LESSON 67

1. *car*
2. *cars*

LESSON 69
1. newspaper
2. movie
3. trombone
4. baseball
5. fish
6. radio
7. building
8. speech
9. wallet
10. deer

LESSON 70
1. predicate nominative
2. direct object
3. direct object
4. direct object
5. direct object
6. predicate nominative
7. direct object
8. direct object
9. predicate nominative
10. predicate nominative

LESSON 71
1. **маши́ну** (direct object)
2. **маши́на** (predicate nominative)
3. **маши́на** (subject)
4. **маши́ну** (direct object)
5. **маши́на** (subject)
6. **маши́на** (subject)
7. **маши́ну** (direct object)
8. **маши́на** (predicate nominative)
9. **маши́ну** (direct object)
10. **маши́на** (predicate nominative)

LESSON 72
1. *I*
2. *I see.*
3. *I do not see.*
4. *car*
5. *cars*
6. *I see the/a car.*
7. *I do not see the/a car.*
8. *I am not a car.*

LESSON 73
1. *Moon*
2. *I see*
3. *I do not see.*
4. *I see the moon.*
5. *I do not see the moon.*
6. *car*
7. *cars*
8. *I see the/a car.*
9. *I do not see the/a car.*
10. *I am not a car.*

LESSON 75
1. *This is/that is the/a car.*
2. *These are/those are (the) cars.*
3. *This is/that is not the/a car.*
4. *These are/those are (the) cars.*
5. *I do not see the moon.*
6. *car*
7. *cars*
8. *I see the/a car.*
9. *This is/that is the moon.*
10. *This is/that is not the moon.*

LESSON 76

1. newspaper
2. newspapers
3. I see the/a newspaper.
4. This is/that is the/a newspaper.
5. These are/those are (the) newspapers.
6. This is/that is the moon.
7. I do not see the moon.
8. This is/that is the/a car.
9. These are/those are not (the) cars.
10. I see the/a car.

LESSON 77

1. I do not see the/a car.
2. I see (the) cars.
3. This is/that is not the/a car.
4. These are/those are (the) cars.
5. I see the/a newspaper.
6. I see (the) newspapers.
7. I do not see the moon.
8. These are/those are not (the) cars.
9. This is/that is the/a newspaper.
10. I see the moon.

LESSON 78

1. These are/those are (the) streets.
2. I see (the) streets.
3. I see the/a car and the/a street.
4. I do not see the/a newspaper.
5. I see (the) newspapers.
6. I see the moon.
7. I am not a car.
8. These are/those are (the) newspapers.
9. This is/that is the moon.
10. I do not see the/a street.

LESSON 79

1. You see the/a street.
2. You do not see (the) streets.
3. You see (the) newspapers.
4. You see the moon.
5. You do not see the/a street.
6. I see the/a car.
7. I see the/a street and (the) cars.
8. This is/that is the/a newspaper.
9. These are/those are not (the) cars.
10. These are/those are (the) streets.

LESSON 80

1. He does not see the/a street.
2. She sees (the) streets.
3. He does not see the/a newspaper.
4. She sees (the) newspapers.
5. He sees (the) streets and (the) cars.
6. He sees the/a car.
7. You see (the) streets.
8. You see the/a newspaper.
9. I see (the) newspapers.
10. This is/that is not the moon.

LESSON 81

1. We see the/a car.
2. We do not see the/a street.
3. We see (the) streets and (the) cars.
4. We see the/a newspaper.
5. We see (the) newspapers.
6. He sees the/a street.
7. She does not see (the) newspapers.
8. You see the moon.
9. I see the/a street and (the) cars.
10. This is/that is the/a newspaper.

LESSON 82

1. Y'all see the/a street and (the) cars.
2. Y'all do not see the/a car.
3. Y'all see (the) newspapers.
4. We see the/a street.
5. We do not see the/a newspaper.
6. She sees the/a newspaper.
7. He sees (the) streets and (the) cars.
8. You see the/a street.
9. I do not see the moon.
10. This is/that is the/a street.

LESSON 83

1. They see the/a car.
2. They do not see (the) newspapers.
3. Y'all see the/a newspaper.
4. Y'all see the/a street.
5. We see (the) streets and (the) cars.
6. She sees (the) streets.
7. He does not see the/a car.
8. You see the moon.
9. I see the/a street and (the) cars.
10. These are/those are (the) streets.

LESSON 86

1. You see Anna.
2. Anna sees the/a car.
3. I see Anna.
4. Anna sees the/a newspaper.
5. Y'all see Anna.
6. This is/that is Anna.
7. They do not see Anna.
8. Anna sees the/a street and (the) cars.
9. He sees Anna.
10. I am Anna.

LESSON 87

1. Hello!
2. Bye!
3. Thank you.
4. Bye, Anna.
5. I see Anna.
6. Hello!
7. We see (the) cars and (the) streets.
8. You see Anna.
9. They see (the) newspapers.
10. This is/that is Anna.

LESSON 88

1. Olga sees Anna.
2. Anna sees Olga.
3. Olga does not see the moon.
4. Clara sees Olga and Anna.
5. They see Clara.
6. Clara sees the/a newspaper.
7. Hello, Olga!
8. This is/that is Clara.
9. Thank you, Olga.
10. Bye!

LESSON 89

1. My name is Anna.
2. My name is Olga.
3. My name is Clara.
4. Thank you, Olga.
5. Bye, Olga.
6. Bye, Anna.
7. This is/that is the/a street.
8. We see (the) streets and (the) cars.
9. Anna does not see the/a car.
10. They see (the) newspapers.

LESSON 90

1. I am reading the/a newspaper.
2. Clara is reading (the) newspapers.
3. We are reading the/a newspaper.
4. You are not reading (the) newspapers.
5. Olga is reading the/a newspaper.
6. My name is Olga.
7. Bye, Clara.
8. Thank you, Anna.
9. Olga sees Clara. Olga does not see Anna.
10. Bye, Anna.

LESSON 94

1. Catherine is reading the/a newspaper.
2. My name is Svetlana.
3. They do not see Natasha.
4. This is/that is Catherine.
5. Svetlana sees Natasha and Catherine.
6. We see Svetlana.
7. Bye, Natasha.
8. This is/that is Olga.
9. Bye, Svetlana.
10. Hello, Olga!

LESSON 96

1. book
2. books
3. I am reading the/a book.
4. You are reading (the) books.
5. She is reading (the) books and (the) newspapers.
6. We are not reading the/a newspaper.
7. My name is Catherine.
8. Thank you, Clara. Bye!
9. Hello. My name is Catherine. This is/that is Olga.
10. Natasha does not see the moon. Y'all see the moon and (the) streets.

LESSON 97

1. Svetlana is buying the/a book.
2. We are not buying the/a car.
3. Catherine is not buying the/a newspaper. She is buying the/a book.
4. Y'all are reading (the) books and (the) newspapers.
5. Hello. My name is Svetlana.
6. They are reading (the) books.
7. These are/those are (the) newspapers. We are reading (the) newspapers.
8. Svetlana sees Catherine and Natasha.
9. I am Catherine. I am not Natasha.
10. You see Olga.

LESSON 98

1. You are buying (the) paper.
2. Svetlana sees (the) books and (the) paper.
3. They do not see (the) paper.
4. These are/those are (the) newspapers. We are reading (the) newspapers.
5. Natasha is reading the/a book.
6. Hello, Catherine.
7. My name is Olga. This is/that is Clara.
8. Y'all are not reading (the) books.
9. They are buying (the) newspapers and (the) books.
10. Thank you, Natasha.

LESSON 100

1. Anna is the/a woman.
2. We are (the) women.
3. We see the/a woman.
4. We see (the) women.
5. They are not (the) women.
6. (The) women are buying (the) books.
7. The/a woman is buying the/a newspaper.
8. You are the/a woman.
9. Catherine and Olga are (the) women.
10. Thank you, Olga. Bye!

LESSON 101

1. Catherine is the/an actress.
2. The women are (the) actresses.
3. They see the/an actress.
4. We do not see (the) actresses.
5. You are the/an actress.
6. Hello. My name is Olga. I am the/an actress.
7. The woman is the/an actress.
8. Natasha and Svetlana are (the) actresses.
9. We are buying (the) paper.
10. I am reading the/a book. Bye!

LESSON 102

1. I am an actress, but you are not an actress.
2. Catherine is an actress, but Natasha is not an actress.
3. We see Svetlana, but we do not see Clara.
4. Natasha reads (the) books, but she does not read (the) newspapers.
5. Y'all are buying the/a car, but we are buying (the) books.
6. Anna is not the/an actress.
7. This is/that is Natasha. She is the/an actress.
8. Y'all do not read (the) newspapers, but y'all are buying the/a newspaper.
9. Catherine and Olga are (the) women.
10. Natasha does not see the women.

LESSON 103

1. Catherine is buying (the) dogs.
2. Y'all do not see the/a dog.
3. This is/that is the/a dog.
4. The/a dog sees Anna.
5. The women see (the) dogs.
6. We are buying the/a dog, but y'all are not buying the/a dog.
7. Svetlana is the/an actress.
8. The actresses see the women.
9. The dogs see (the) paper.
10. The women are reading (the) books. They are not reading (the) newspapers.

LESSON 104

1. Anna is the/a (female) student.
2. The women are (the) (female) students.
3. We see (the) (female) students.
4. The/a dog is not the/a (female) student!
5. Natasha is a (female) student, but Clara is not a (female) student.
6. (The) (female) students are buying (the) books.
7. The/an actress sees (the) dogs.
8. The actress is a woman.
9. This is/that is the/a (female) student.
10. I am reading the/a book.

LESSON 105

1. Olga is the/a (female) journalist, but Catherine is the/an actress.
2. I see (the) (female) journalists.
3. Y'all do not see the/a (female) journalist.
4. Clara is not the/a (female) journalist.
5. Catherine is a woman and a (female) journalist.
6. (The) dogs see the/a woman.
7. Anna is a (female) student and an actress.
8. We are not (the) (female) students. Bye!
9. The/a woman is reading the/a book.
10. This is/that is Natasha. She is the/a (female) journalist.

LESSON 106

1. Olga is the/a (female) athlete.
2. Clara and Anna are (the) (female) athletes.
3. Svetlana sees the/a (female) athlete.
4. The/a (female) journalist sees (the) (female) athletes.
5. Y'all do not see (the) (female) students.
6. (The) dogs see (the) actresses.
7. These are/those are Catherine and Natasha. They are (the) (female) students.
8. We see (the) (female) journalists.
9. Y'all are (the) women.
10. You are the/a (female) athlete, but I am the/an actress.

LESSON 108

1. This is/that is the/a (female) journalist's newspaper.
2. My name is Natasha. I am buying Olga's car.
3. Clara and the/an actress are reading Catherine's book.
4. The women see the/an actress's dog.
5. The/a (female) athlete is reading Svetlana's book.
6. (The) (female) journalists see Anna's street.
7. (The) (female) students are reading the/a (female) athlete's book.
8. We do not see (the) (female) students.
9. This is/that is Olga. She is buying Clara's dog.
10. Clara is the/a (female) journalist, but she does not read (the) newspapers.

LESSON 109

1. These are/those are (the) women's dogs.
2. These are/those are (the) actresses' cars.
3. Y'all see the (female) journalists' newspaper.
4. Hello. We do not see the (female) students' cars.
5. The/a (female) student is reading Anna's book.
6. The/a woman's dogs see the moon.
7. My name is Natasha. I am the/an actress.
8. I am the/a (female) journalist, but I do not read (female) journalists' books.
9. You are buying Clara's newspaper.
10. This is/that is the (female) students' paper.

LESSON 110

1. This is/that is the/a girl.
2. Natasha and Svetlana are girls.
3. the/a girl's book
4. the girls' book
5. We see the/a girl.
6. The/a (female) journalist sees (the) girls.
7. They do not see the/a girl's dog.
8. (The) girls are reading (the) books.
9. The girls are (the) (female) athletes.
10. Clara is the/a (female) student, but Anna is the/an actress.

LESSON 111

1. This is/that is the/a cat.
2. These are/those are (the) cats.
3. This is/that is the/a girl's cat.
4. The/a dog sees Olga's cat.
5. You are not the/a dog. You are the/a cat!
6. The/a cat sees the/a girl.
7. The/a girl's dog sees the/a cat.
8. (The) girls are reading the (female) athletes' book.
9. The women are (the) (female) students. They are not (the) actresses.
10. The girls see the/a dog, but they do not see the/a cat.

LESSON 112

1. *This is/that is (the/a) grandmother's cat.*
2. *Natasha is Anna's grandmother.*
3. *(The/a) grandmother sees (the) girls, but the girls do not see (the) grandmother.*
4. *The/a girl's cat sees the/a dog.*
5. *The/a (female) journalist is buying the/a cat.*
6. *The girls' cats see (the) dogs.*
7. *My name is Svetlana. I am a (female) athlete and a (female) student.*
8. *The/a cat is not reading the/a newspaper!*
9. *Y'all do not see the/a cat.*
10. *This is/that is not the/a dog!*

LESSON 113

1. *These are/those are (the) girls' pens.*
2. *This is/that is the/a (female) journalist's pen.*
3. *We do not see Natasha's pens.*
4. *Y'all are reading Catherine's book.*
5. *These are/those are (the) (female) students. They are reading (the) (female) journalists' newspapers.*
6. *Thank you, Olga. My name is Anna.*
7. *Clara and Catherine are buying the/a girl's newspapers.*
8. *This is/that is Clara's dog. Clara is the/a (female) student.*
9. *I am the/a grandmother, but you are the/a (female) athlete.*
10. *I am the/a (female) journalist, but I do not read books.*

LESSON 114

1. *This is/that is the/a girl's food.*
2. *This is/that is the/a dog's food.*
3. *This is/that is (the) dogs' food.*
4. *The/a cat sees Svetlana's food.*
5. *We are buying (the) food, but y'all are buying (the) books.*
6. *The/a grandmother is buying (the) food, but the girls are buying (the) newspapers.*
7. *The/a woman sees (the) pens, but she does not see (the) books.*
8. *We are not reading the (female) athletes' book.*
9. *Hello, Catherine and Natasha!*
10. *This is/that is not Clara's car. This is/that is Anna's car.*

LESSON 115

1. *I am giving (the) food.*
2. *You are giving the/a book.*
3. *He is giving the/a pen.*
4. *(The/a) grandmother is giving the/a newspaper.*
5. *We are giving (the) books and (the) pens.*
6. *Y'all are giving the/a car.*
7. *They are giving (the) food.*
8. *This is/that is the/a cat's food.*
9. *These are/those are (the) girls' books.*
10. *Y'all see (the) (female) students, but we do not see (the) (female) students.*

LESSON 116

1. direct object: *money*
   indirect object: *friend*
2. direct object: *money*
   indirect object: *charity*
3. direct object: *example*
   indirect object: *class*
4. direct object: *tea*
   indirect object: *Mom*
5. direct object: *gift*
   indirect object: *teacher*
6. direct object: *sandwiches*
   indirect object: *us*
7. direct object: *story*
   indirect object: *judge*
8. direct object: *song*
   indirect object: *audience*
9. direct object: *copies*
   indirect object: *everyone*
10. direct object: *shirt*
    indirect object: *me*

LESSON 117

1. *(The) (female) students are giving food to the/a cat.*
2. *Svetlana is giving the/a pen to the/a girl.*
3. *We are giving the/a book to the/a (female) student.*
4. *You are not giving (the) paper to the/a woman.*
5. *Y'all are giving (the) pens to the/an actress.*
6. *(The) (female) athletes are reading (the) newspapers.*
7. *These are/those are (the) (female) journalists' pens.*
8. *I am not giving the/a newspaper to Svetlana. She is not the/a (female) journalist.*
9. *This is/that is the/a girl's cat.*
10. *Olga's dog sees (the) cats.*

LESSON 118

1. *Catherine is giving (the) pens to (the) (female) journalists.*
2. *He is giving (the) food to (the) dogs and (the) cats.*
3. *I am giving Clara's pen to Anna.*
4. *The/a grandmother is giving (the) books to (the) girls.*
5. *We are giving (the) dogs to Catherine.*
6. *(The) women are giving (the) food to the/a (female) student.*
7. *This is/that is Svetlana. She is giving (the) food to (the) cats.*
8. *He is not buying the/a newspaper. He is buying the/a book.*
9. *This is/that is the/a dog's food.*
10. *I am the/a dog, but you are the/a cat.*

LESSON 119

1. *She is showing (the) food to the/a dog.*
2. *The/an actress is showing the/a book to (the) (female) journalists.*
3. *The/a girl is showing the/a dog to the/a (female) athlete.*
4. *You are showing the/an actress's car to (the) women.*
5. *Y'all are showing (the) food to (the) cats.*
6. *He is showing (the) food to (the) dogs, but he is not giving (the) food to (the) dogs.*
7. *We are showing the/a pen to the/a (female) journalist.*
8. *I am giving (the) paper to Clara.*
9. *Y'all are reading (the/a) grandmother's book.*
10. *The/a dog sees Anna's food!*

LESSON 122

1. *This is/that is Catherine's purse.*
2. *We are showing the/a purse to Olga and Natasha.*
3. *The/a woman is showing (the) purses to (the) actresses.*
4. *These are/those are (the) (female) students' purses.*
5. *The/a (female) journalist is giving the/a pen to the/a (female) student.*
6. *Y'all are reading Clara's newspaper.*
7. *Olga and Catherine are giving (the) food to (the) dogs.*
8. *He is not buying (the) books. He is buying (the) food.*
9. *I am showing the/a book to Natasha, but I am not giving the/a book to Natasha.*
10. *This is/that is Clara's grandmother.*

LESSON 123

1. *Anna is showing (the) cars to me.*
2. *She sees me.*
3. *The girl is giving the/a purse to me.*
4. *The dogs do not see me.*
5. *Anna's grandmother is giving (the) food to (the) girls.*
6. *The/a girl's cat sees (the) food.*
7. *This is/that is Clara's food. This is/that is not the/a dog's food.*
8. *The woman is the/an actress.*
9. *Y'all are giving the/a book to Natasha.*
10. *They are showing the/a dog to Olga.*

LESSON 125

1. *Natasha is showing the/a library to (the) (female) students.*
2. *We are giving (the) books to the/a library.*
3. *Catherine is giving the/a book to me.*
4. *These are/those are not the libraries' books.*
5. *The/an actress sees me!*
6. *The/a (female) journalist is giving the/a book to me.*
7. *This is/that is the/a library's book.*
8. *They are buying (the) food, but we are buying (the) purses.*
9. *The/a woman is showing the/a purse to me, but I am not buying the/a purse.*
10. *Y'all are giving (the) paper to (the) (female) students.*

LESSON 127

1. *I like (the) cats.*
2. *I like the purse.*
3. *I like (the) libraries and (the) books.*
4. *The/a woman is showing the/a purse to Catherine.*
5. *Catherine's grandmother is giving (the) food to the/a cat.*
6. *Svetlana is Natasha's grandmother.*
7. *They see the/a girl's dog.*
8. *This is/that is Olga's pen.*
9. *He is giving the/a cat to Clara.*
10. *You are giving (the) pens to (the) (female) students.*

LESSON 128

1. *I like (the) books, but I don't like (the) libraries.*
2. *The/a woman is showing the/a purse to me, but I don't like the purse.*
3. *Svetlana's dog sees me. I don't like Svetlana's dog.*
4. *They see the/an actress.*
5. *Olga's grandmother is giving (the) food to me.*
6. *My name is Clara. I like (the) cats.*
7. *Y'all are giving Catherine's book to Natasha.*
8. *You are not the/a cat. You are the/a dog.*
9. *We are showing (the) purses to (the) women.*
10. *He is giving (the) pens to (the) (female) students.*

LESSON 129

1. *(The) dogs don't like the woman.*
2. *Svetlana likes the purse, but Natasha doesn't like the purse.*
3. *The actresses like (the) cars.*
4. *The (female) students like (the) libraries.*
5. *The/a dog likes (the) cats.*
6. *The/a dog likes the/a girl.*
7. *I like (the) dogs, but Catherine likes (the) cats.*
8. *The/a cat likes the/a car.*
9. *The/a woman is giving (the) food to (the) cats, but the cats don't like the food.*
10. *The/a dog doesn't like the/a cat!*

LESSON 130

1. Preposition: *behind*
   Object of preposition: *couch*
2. Preposition: *beside*
   Object of preposition: *lamp*
3. Preposition: *in*
   Object of preposition: *trunk*
4. Preposition: *through*
   Object of preposition: *tunnel*
5. Preposition: *under*
   Object of preposition: *house*
6. Preposition: *before*
   Object of preposition: *lunch*
7. Preposition: *after*
   Object of preposition: *school*
8. Preposition: *by*
   Object of preposition: *post office*
9. Preposition: *on*
   Object of preposition: *campus*
10. Preposition: *beyond*
    Object of preposition: *mountain*

LESSON 131

1. *Clara is at the/a library.*
2. *Catherine and Olga are at the/a library.*
3. *He is at the/a library, but she is not at the/a library.*
4. *(The) books and (the) newspapers are at the/a library.*
5. *The/a (female) journalist is at the/a library.*
6. *I don't like (the) libraries. I don't like (the) books.*
7. *Y'all are showing the/a library to Natasha.*
8. *I like (the) cats, but Olga doesn't like (the) cats.*
9. *We are showing the/a library to (the) (female) students. The (female) students like the library.*
10. *These are/those are (the) girls' books.*

LESSON 132

1. *(The) books are at (the) libraries.*
2. *We read (the) books at (the) libraries.*
3. *The/a car is at the/a library.*
4. *The girls like (the) books.*
5. *I don't like Catherine's car, but I like Olga's car.*
6. *Natasha's grandmother is giving (the) food to me.*
7. *The dogs see me!*
8. *I am reading (the) newspapers at the/a library.*
9. *(The) women are buying (the) purses.*
10. *The/a girl's dogs like (the) food.*

LESSON 133

1. *(The) girls are at (the/a) school.*
2. *(The) girls are at (the) schools.*
3. *Olga is at (the/a) school. Olga doesn't like (the) school.*
4. *The/a dog is not at (the/a) school.*
5. *Anna is at the/a library, but Svetlana is at (the/a) school.*
6. *(The) women are at (the) libraries.*
7. *We are showing the/a school to (the) (female) journalists. (The) (female) journalists like the school.*
8. *Y'all are giving (the) pens and (the) paper to (the) schools.*
9. *(The) dogs like the/a car.*
10. *Anna's grandmother likes the food.*

LESSON 134

1. *Clara and Svetlana work at the/a library.*
2. *The/a woman works at the/a school.*
3. *Y'all work at (the) libraries.*
4. *You work at the/a school, but I work at the/a library.*
5. *(The) dogs like the car.*
6. *Catherine sees me, but I do not see Catherine.*
7. *We are showing Clara's school to (the) girls.*
8. *Olga's cat does not like the food.*
9. *Svetlana does not like (the) books. She is giving (the) books to the/a library.*
10. *I like (the) dogs, but Natasha likes (the) cats.*

LESSON 135

1. *Where is the cat?*
2. *Where does Natasha work?*
3. *Where are Anna and Olga?*
4. *Where do y'all work?*
5. *We work at (the) schools, but Anna works at (the) libraries.*
6. *I am at (the/a) school, but Clara is not at (the/a) school.*
7. *Natasha's grandmother is giving (the) food to Natasha.*
8. *The/a cat sees me. I don't like (the) cats.*
9. *The girls don't like Anna's car.*
10. *This is/that is the/a cat.*

LESSON 136

1. Svetlana's grandmother is at the/a hospital.
2. Olga works at the/a hospital.
3. You do not work at the/a hospital.
4. Where do you work? I work at (the) hospitals.
5. Where is Olga? She is not at the/a library.
6. Catherine is buying the/a dog.
7. The women work at the/a hospital.
8. The girls don't like the hospital.
9. My name is Anna. I work at the/a library.
10. Natasha and Clara are giving (the) books to (the) libraries and (the) hospitals.

LESSON 139

1. Anna is at (the/a) school.
2. Anna is going to (the/a) school.
3. Catherine is at the/a hospital.
4. Catherine is going to the/a hospital.
5. Where is Clara's grandmother? She is not at the/a hospital.
6. I am going to the/a library.
7. I am at the/a library.
8. Catherine and Svetlana are going to the/a hospital.
9. Clara likes (the) dogs, but Svetlana likes (the) cats.
10. We are going to the/a library.

LESSON 140

1. yes
2. no
3. no
4. yes
5. no
6. yes
7. yes
8. yes
9. no
10. no

LESSON 142

1. You are writing with the/a pen.
2. The/a (female) student is writing with the/a pen.
3. Olga and Catherine are writing with the/a pen.
4. We are writing.
5. Y'all are writing, but we are reading.
6. Where is the/a pen?
7. Clara works at the/a hospital, but Anna works at the/a library.
8. I am not writing with the/a pen. I don't like (the) pens.
9. The/a girl doesn't like (the) school.
10. The (female) students don't like Anna's book.

LESSON 143

1. *(The) girls are writing with (the) pens.*
2. *(The) (female) students are writing with (the) pens.*
3. *Clara is not writing with the/a pen. Clara doesn't like (the) pens.*
4. *We are writing with (the) pens.*
5. *Anna and Natasha work at the/a hospital.*
6. *The girls are going to (the/a) school.*
7. *The girls are at (the/a) school. The girls don't like (the) school.*
8. *Where does Catherine work?*
9. *Catherine and Natasha work at the/a library.*
10. *(The) women are showing (the) purses to me, but I don't like (the) purses.*

LESSON 146

1. *I do not have the/a cat. I have the/a dog.*
2. *The/a dog doesn't have (the) food.*
3. *The/a cat has the/a dog's food!*
4. *Anna is going to (the/a) school. Clara is at (the/a) school.*
5. *I do not have the/a purse. The/a woman is showing the/a purse to me.*
6. *Natasha's grandmother has the/a dog.*
7. *(The) dogs do not see me.*
8. *Where do (the) (female) athletes work?*
9. *My name is Olga. This is/that is Catherine.*
10. *We are not at the/a library.*

LESSON 145

1. *I have the/a dog.*
2. *I have the/a purse.*
3. *I have the/a cat. I like cats.*
4. *I have the/a car.*
5. *Natasha likes the/a car, but Anna doesn't like the car.*
6. *We are writing with (the) pens.*
7. *The/a cat is at the/a library.*
8. *Where are (the) (female) journalists?*
9. *Y'all do not see Clara's grandmother.*
10. *The/an actress is buying the/a car.*

GLOSSARY

а *but, and*

актри́са *actress*

ба́бушка *grandmother*

библиоте́ка *library*

бизнесме́н *businessperson*

больни́ца *hospital*

бума́га *paper*

в *to* (with accusative); *at, in* (with prepositional)

вас *you* (accusative)

ви́жу *I see*

вы *y'all* (in informal speech); *you* (in formal speech)

газе́та *newspaper*

где *where*

даю́ *I give*

диплома́т *diplomat*

до свида́ния *goodbye*

до́брое у́тро *good morning*

до́брый ве́чер *good evening*

до́брый день *good day*

еда́ *food*

есть *there is*

же́нщина *woman*

журнали́ст *journalist*

журнали́стка *female journalist*

здра́вствуй *hello*

здра́вствуйте *hello* (formal)

зову́т *they call*

и *and*

иду́ *I go*

инжене́р *engineer*

как *how?*

кни́га *book*

ко́шка *cat*

Луна́ *moon*

маши́на *car*

меня́ *me*

мне *to me, for me*

мы *we*

не *not*

нет *no, there is not*

но *but*

нра́вится *he/she/it is pleasing*

нра́вятся *they are pleasing*

он *he*

она́ *she*

они́ *they*

пило́т *pilot*

пишу́ *I write*

пожа́луйста *you're welcome*

пока́ *bye!*

пока́зываю *I show*

покупа́ю *I buy*

приве́т *hello* (informal)

рабо́таю *I work*

ру́чка *pen*

соба́ка *dog*

спаси́бо *thank you*

спортсме́нка *female athlete*

студе́нт *male university student*

студе́нтка *female university student*

су́мка *purse*

ты *you*

у *by* (with genitive)

у́лица *street*

чита́ю *I read*

шко́ла *school*

э́то *this is, that is, these are, those are*

я *I*